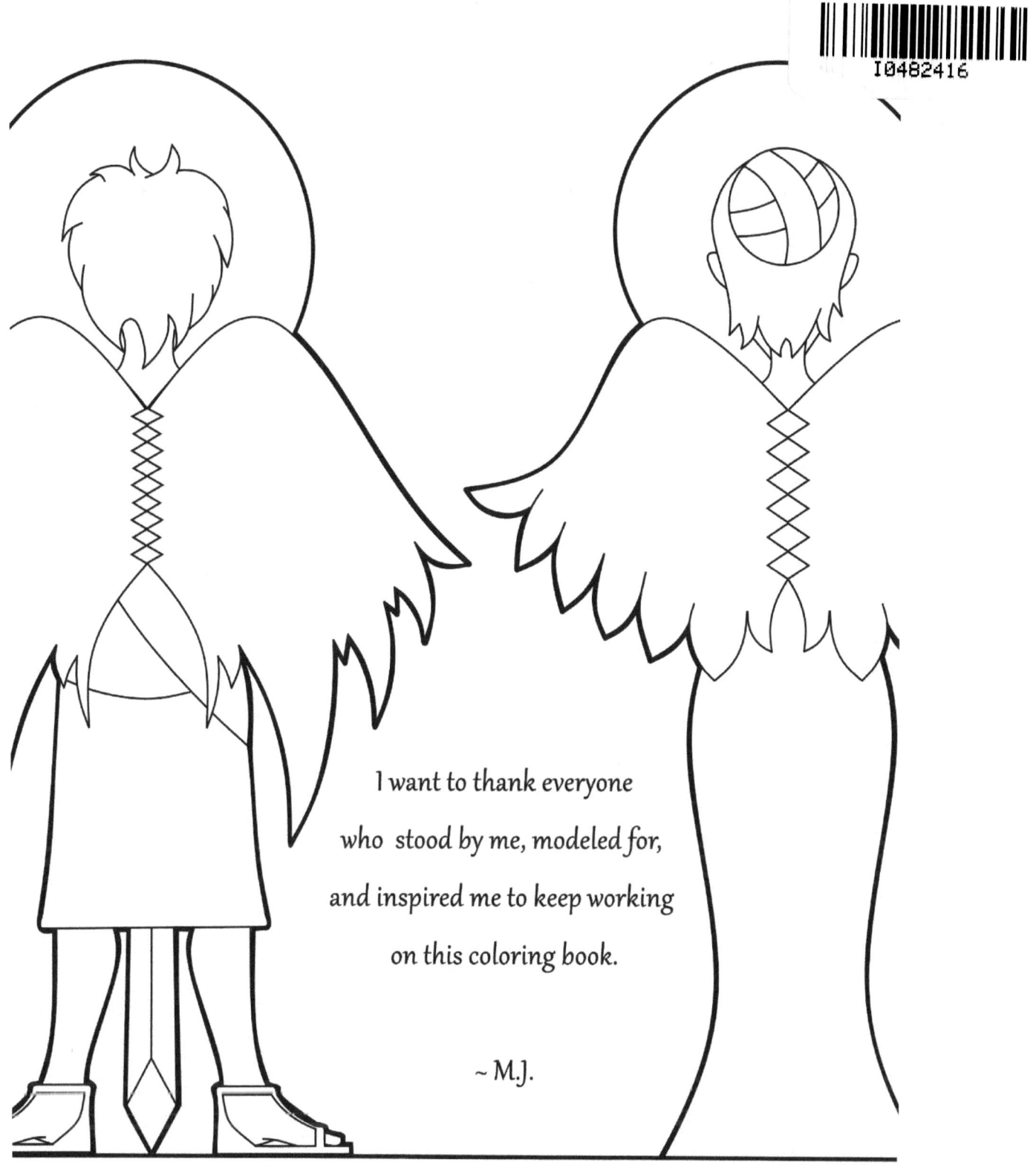

I want to thank everyone

who stood by me, modeled for,

and inspired me to keep working

on this coloring book.

~ M.J.

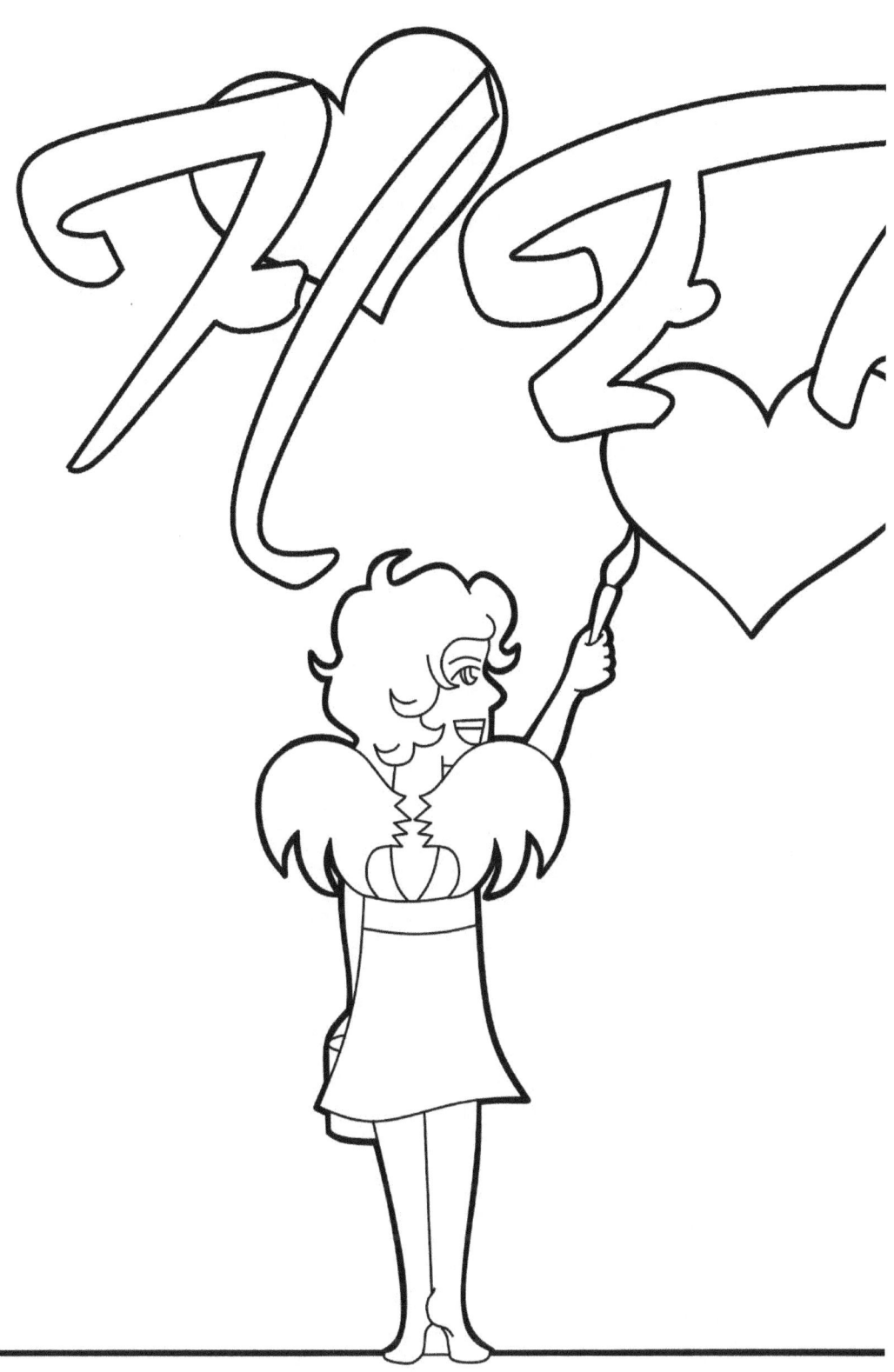

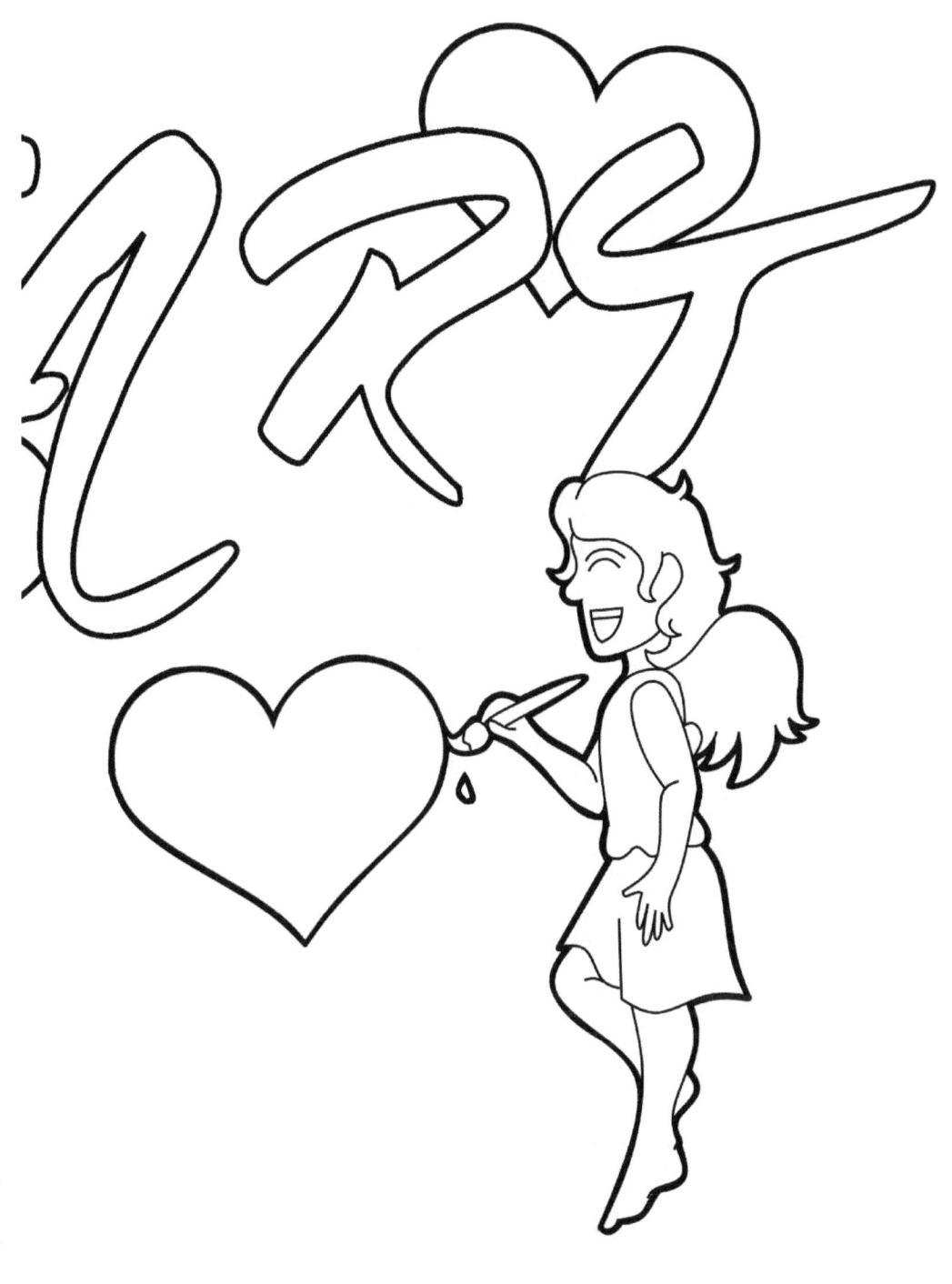

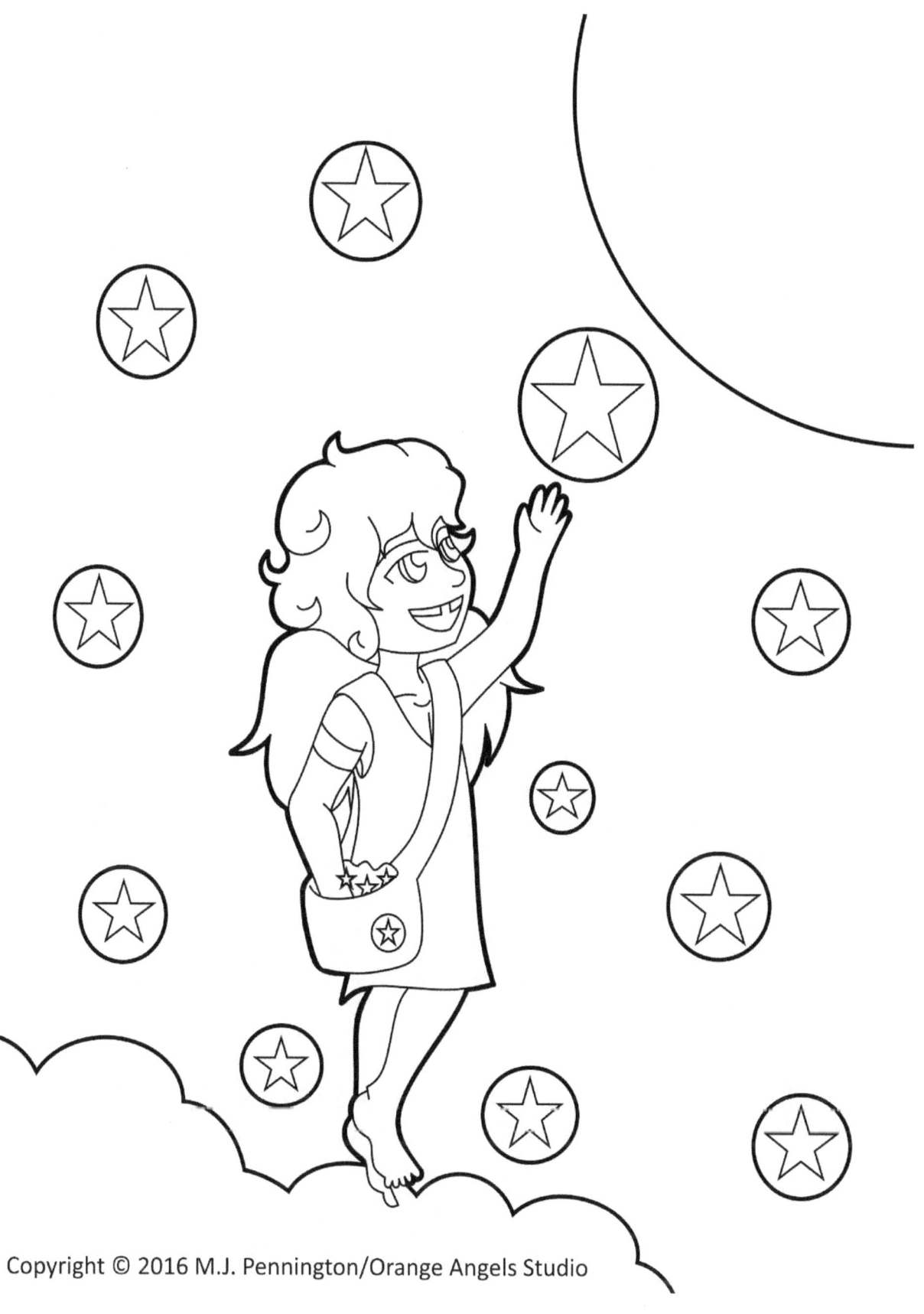

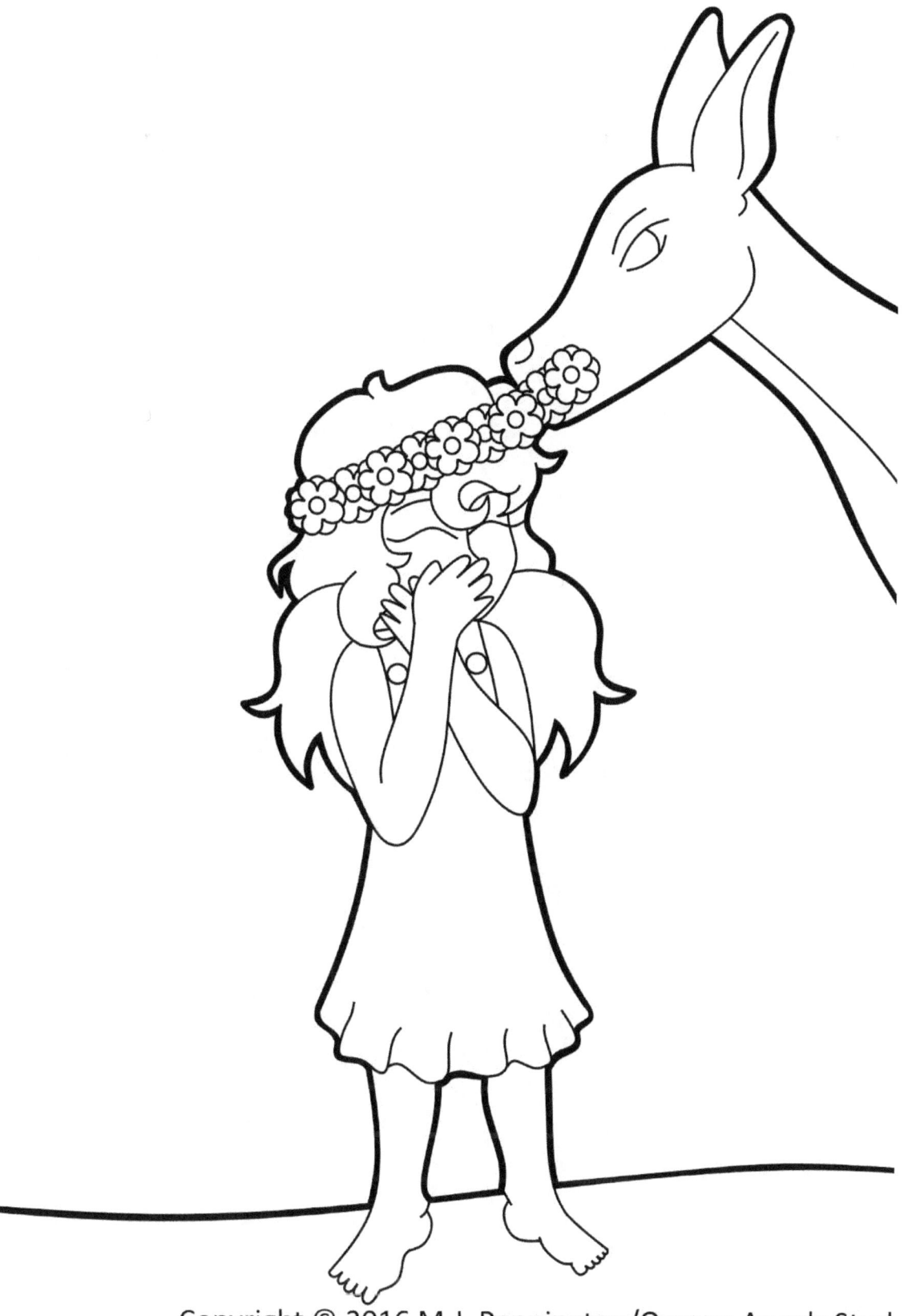

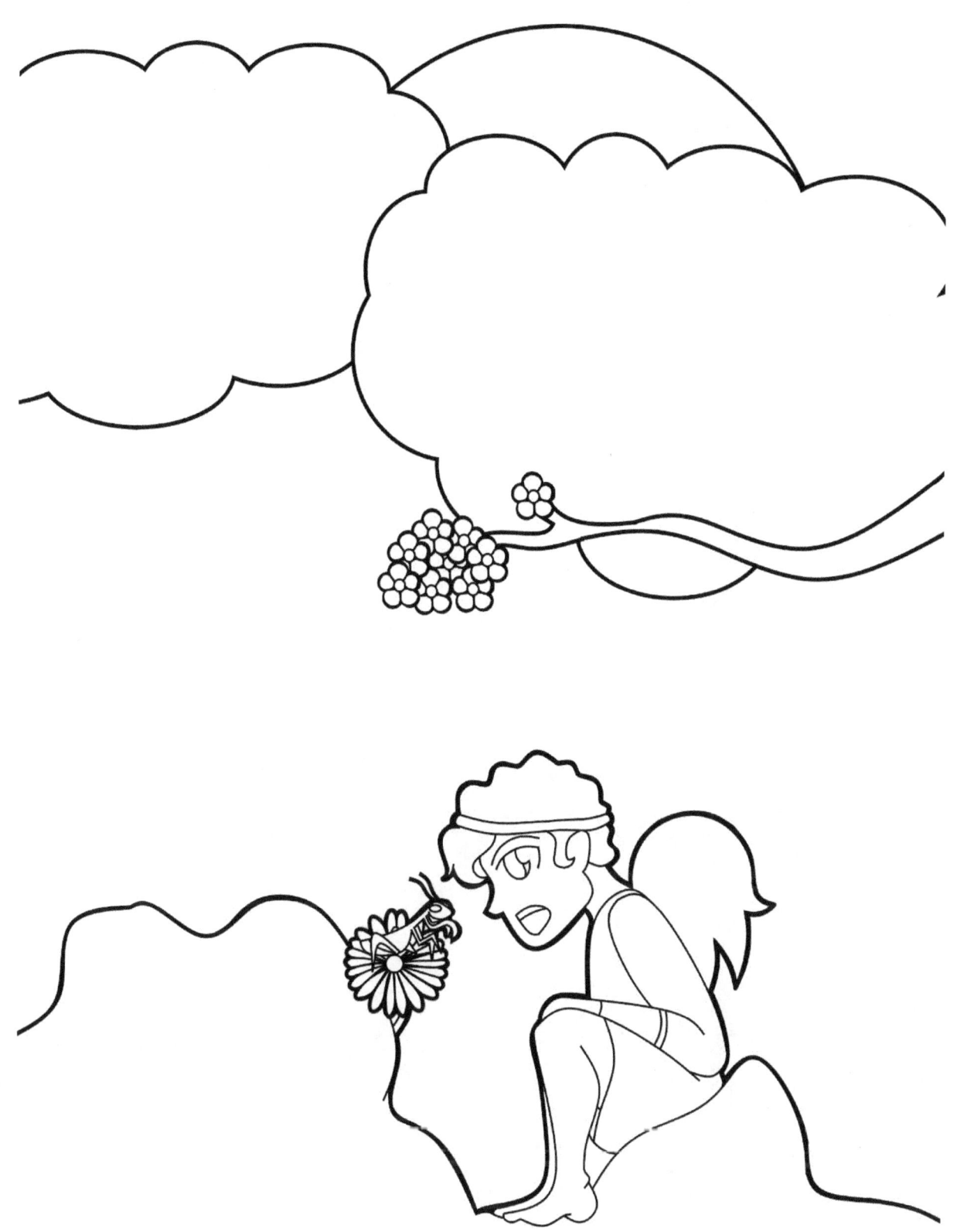

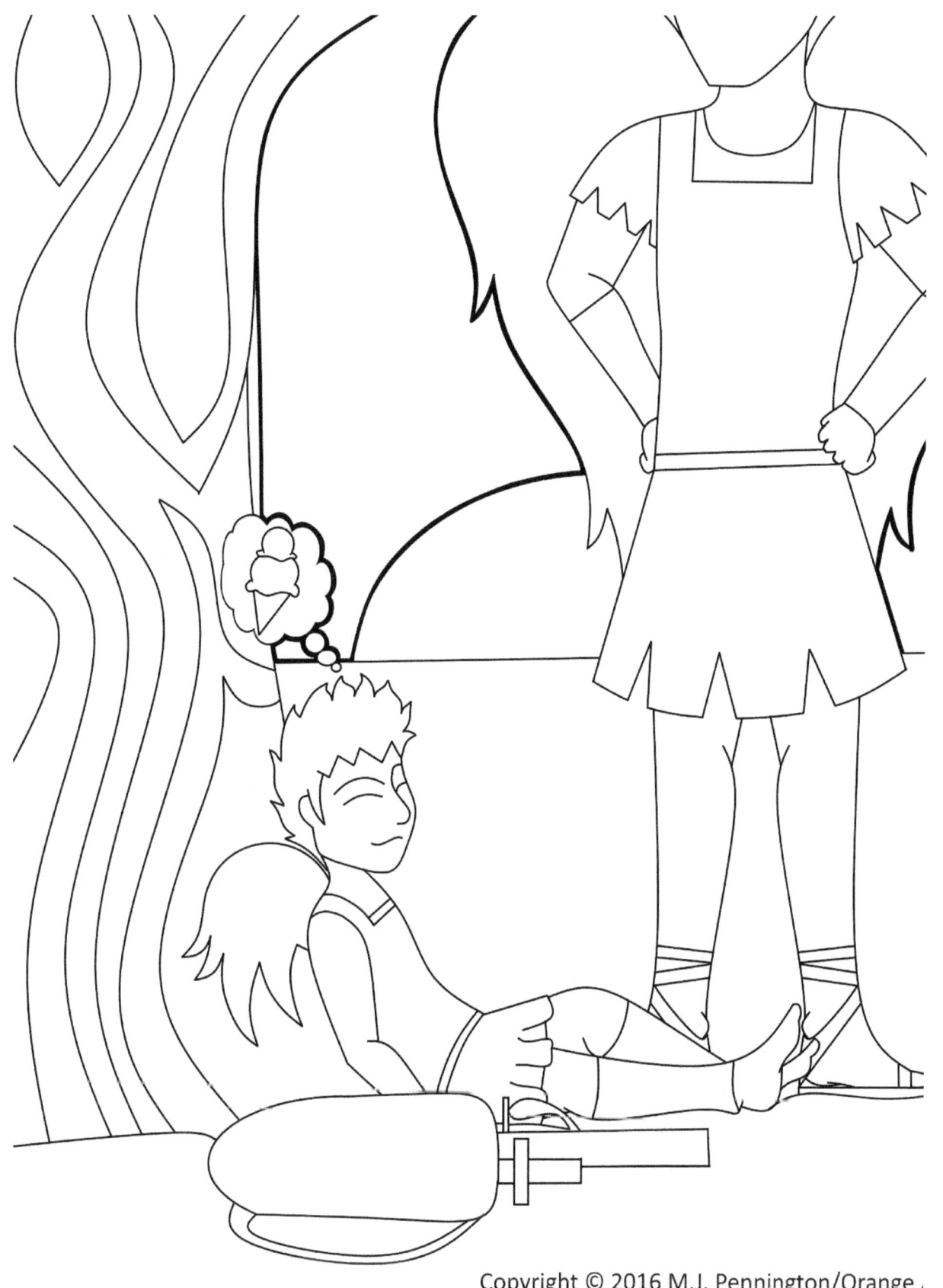

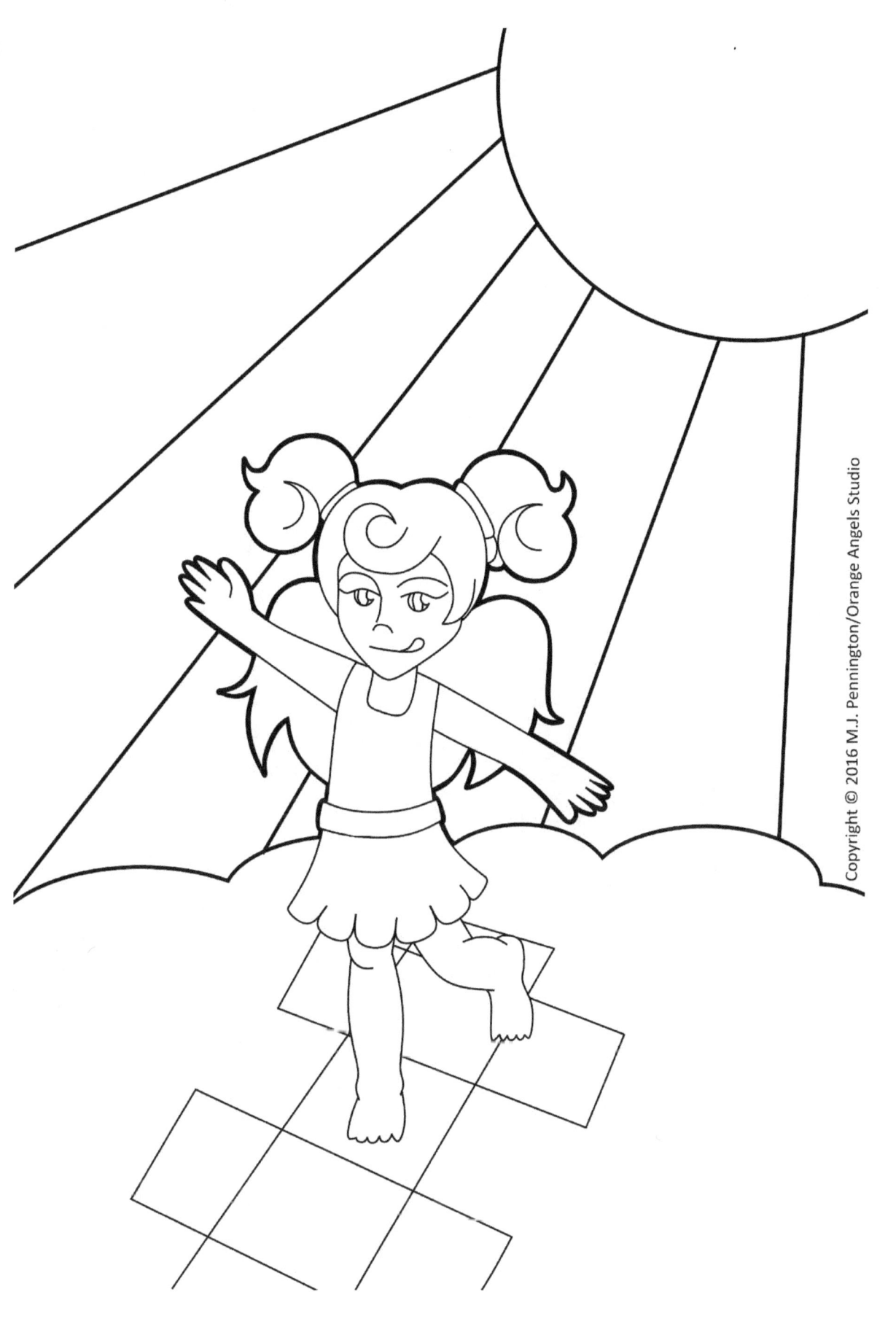

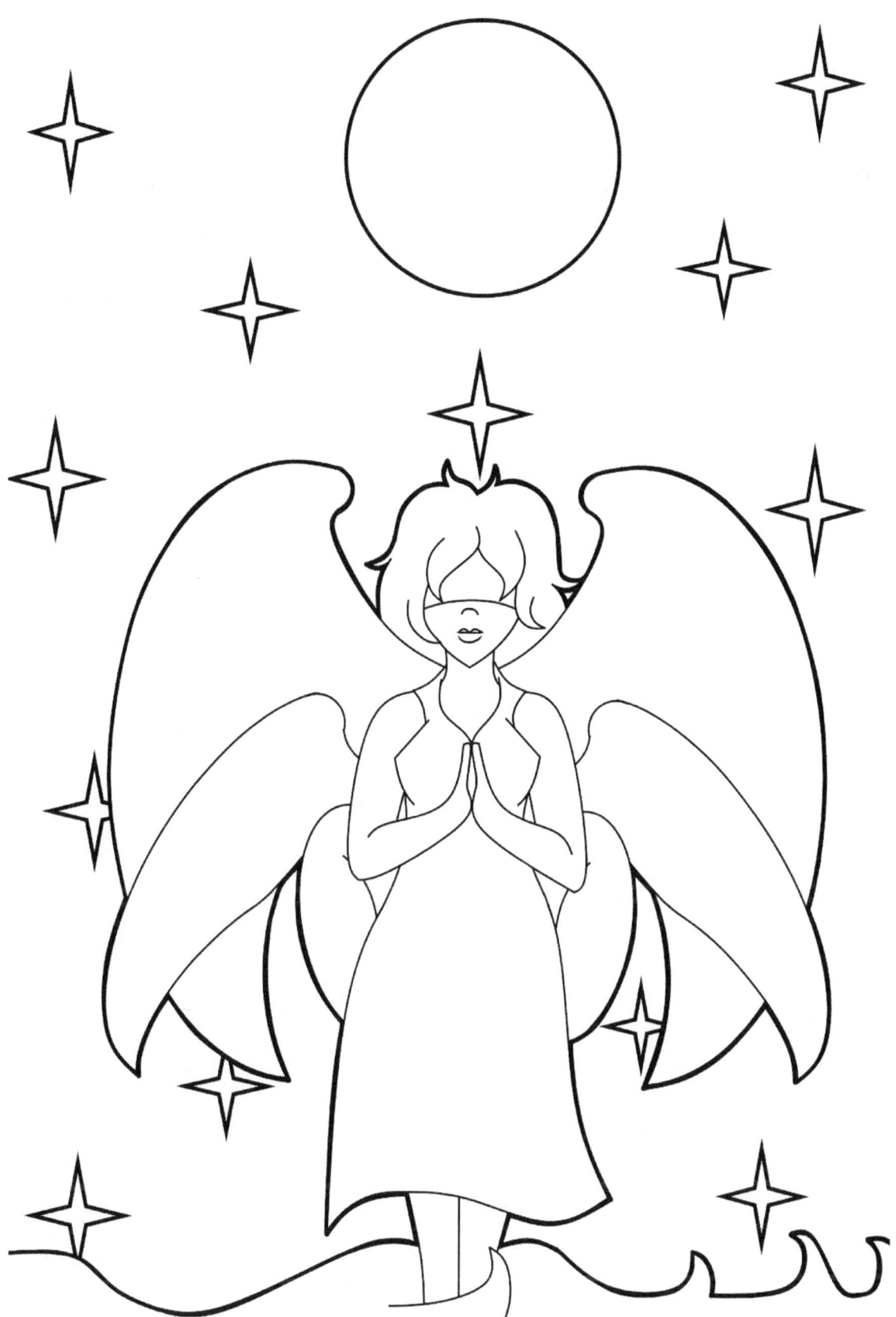

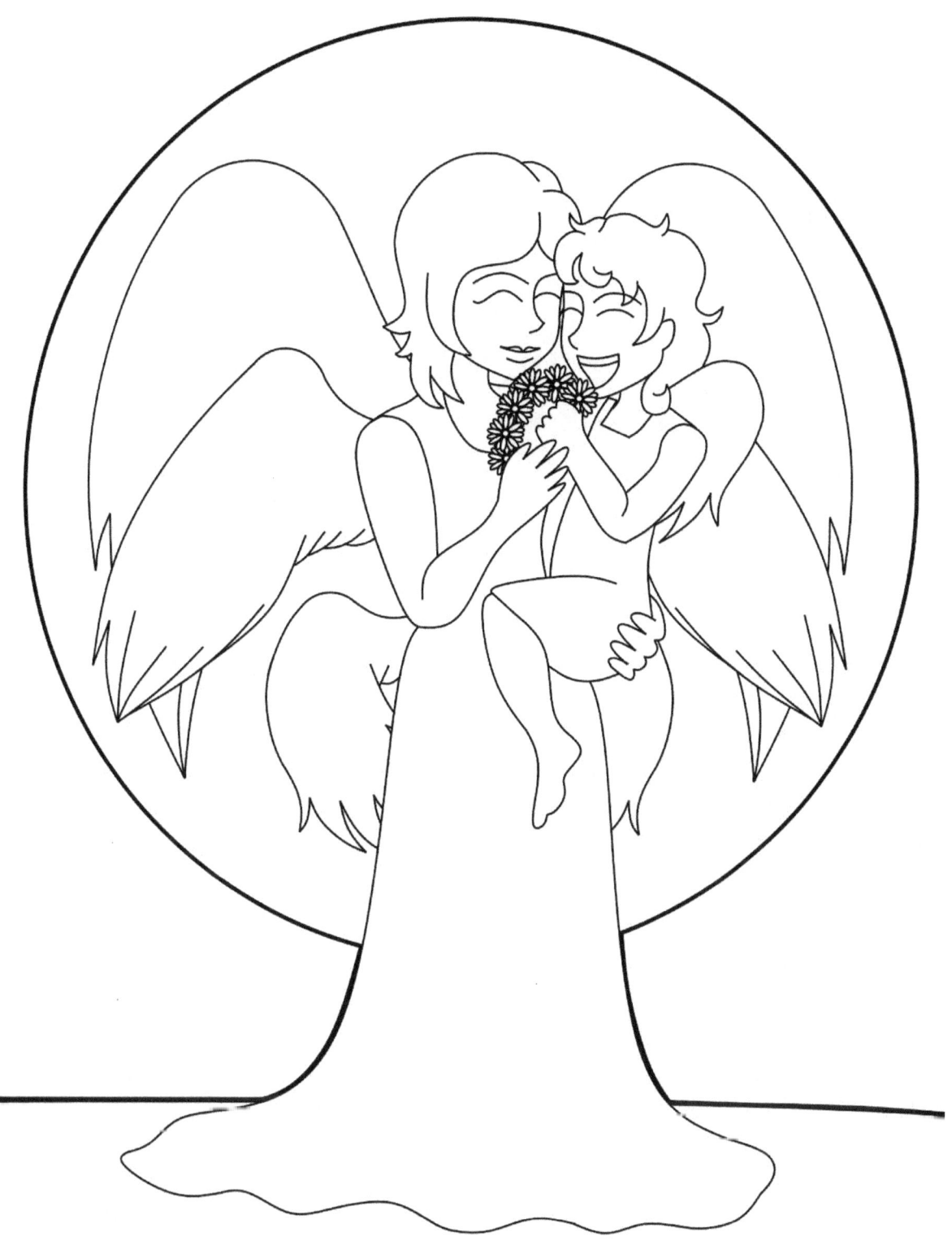

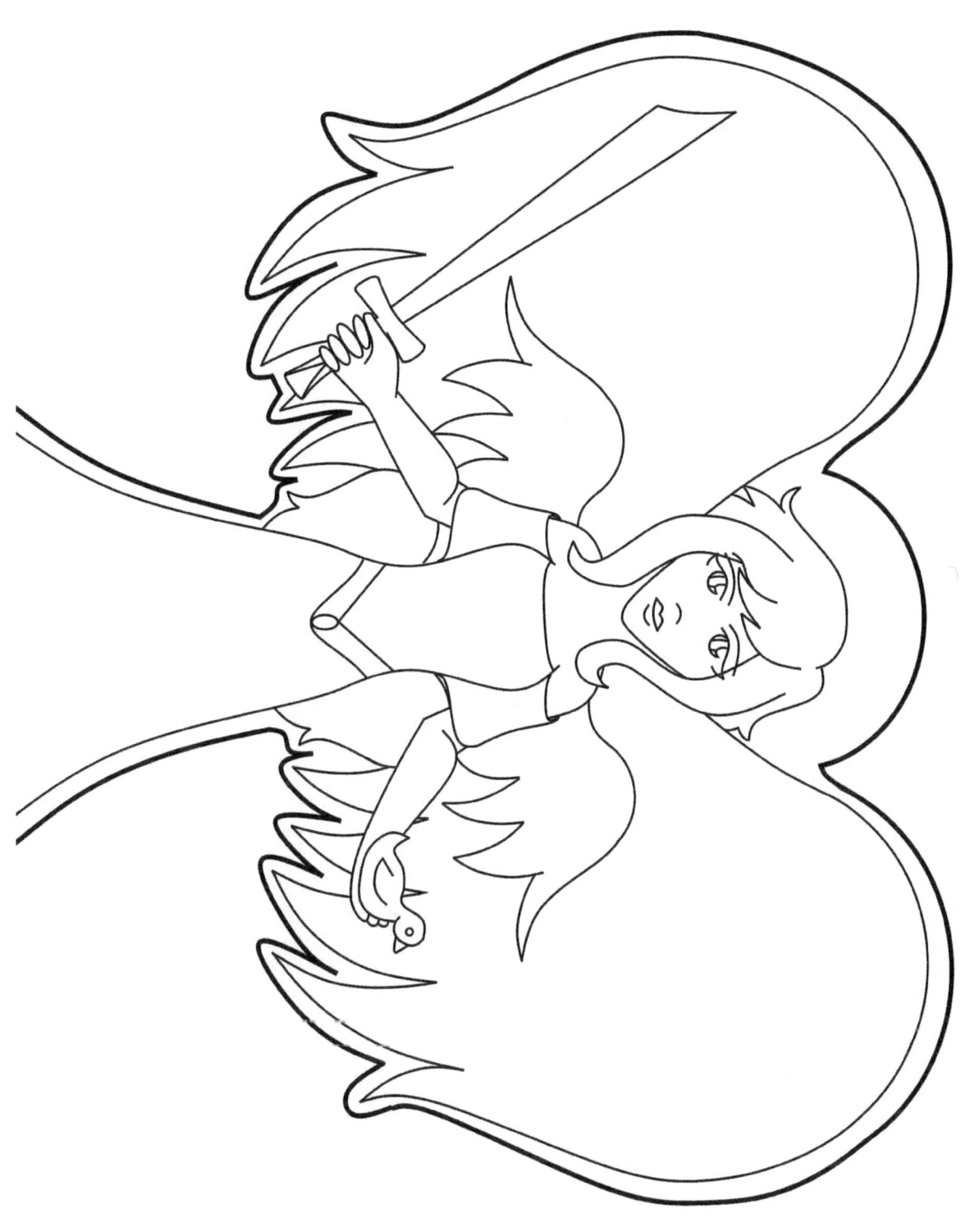

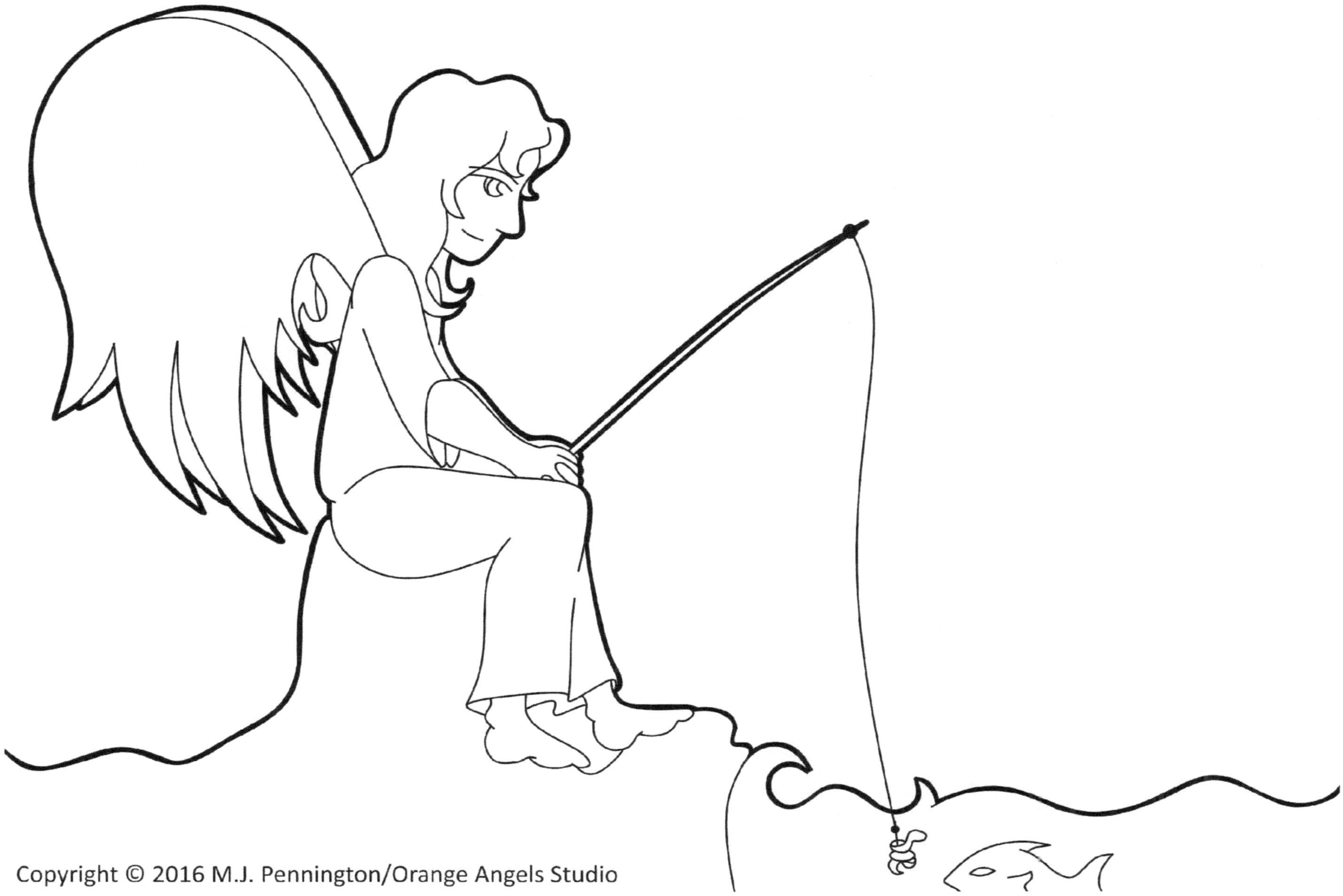

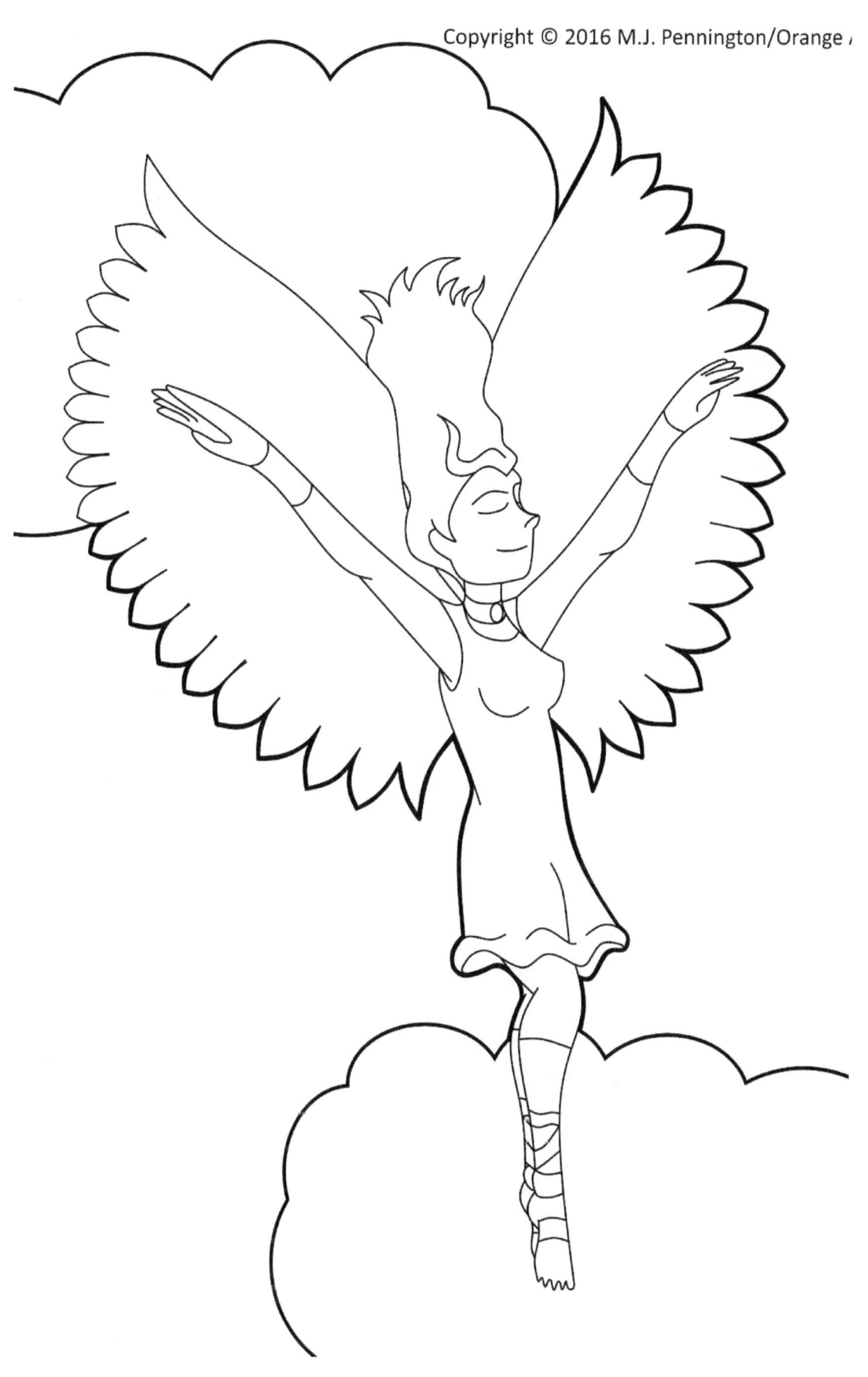

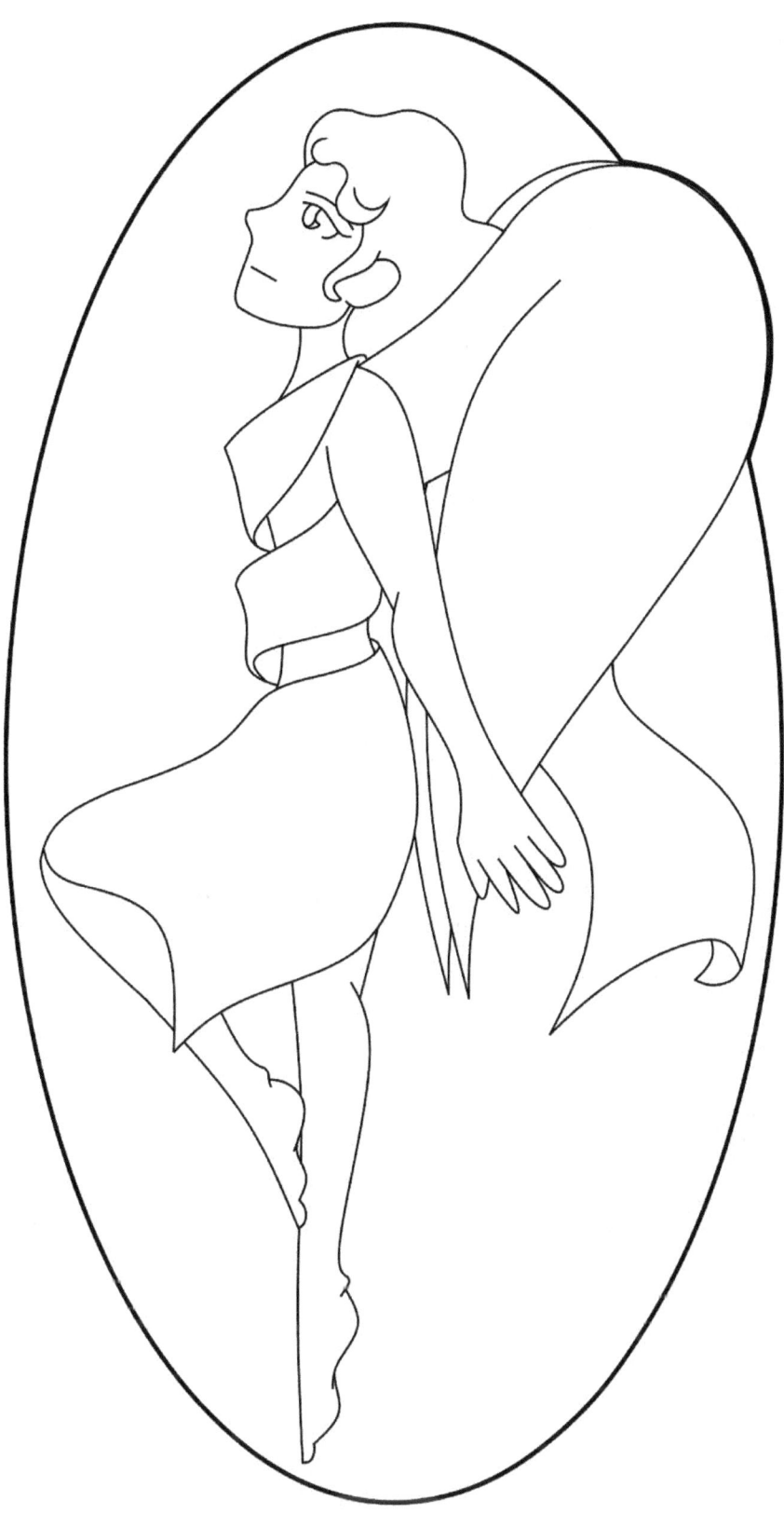

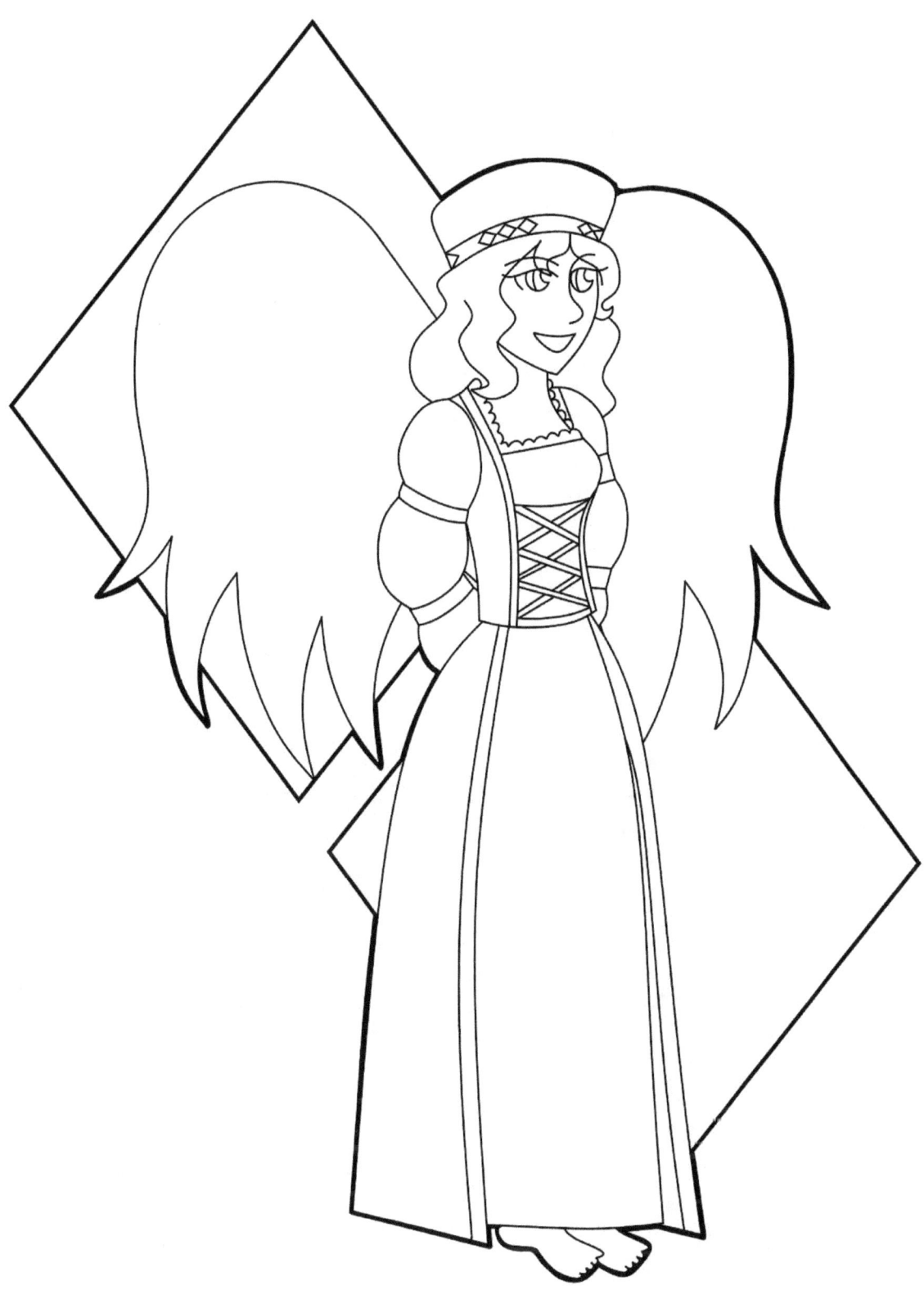

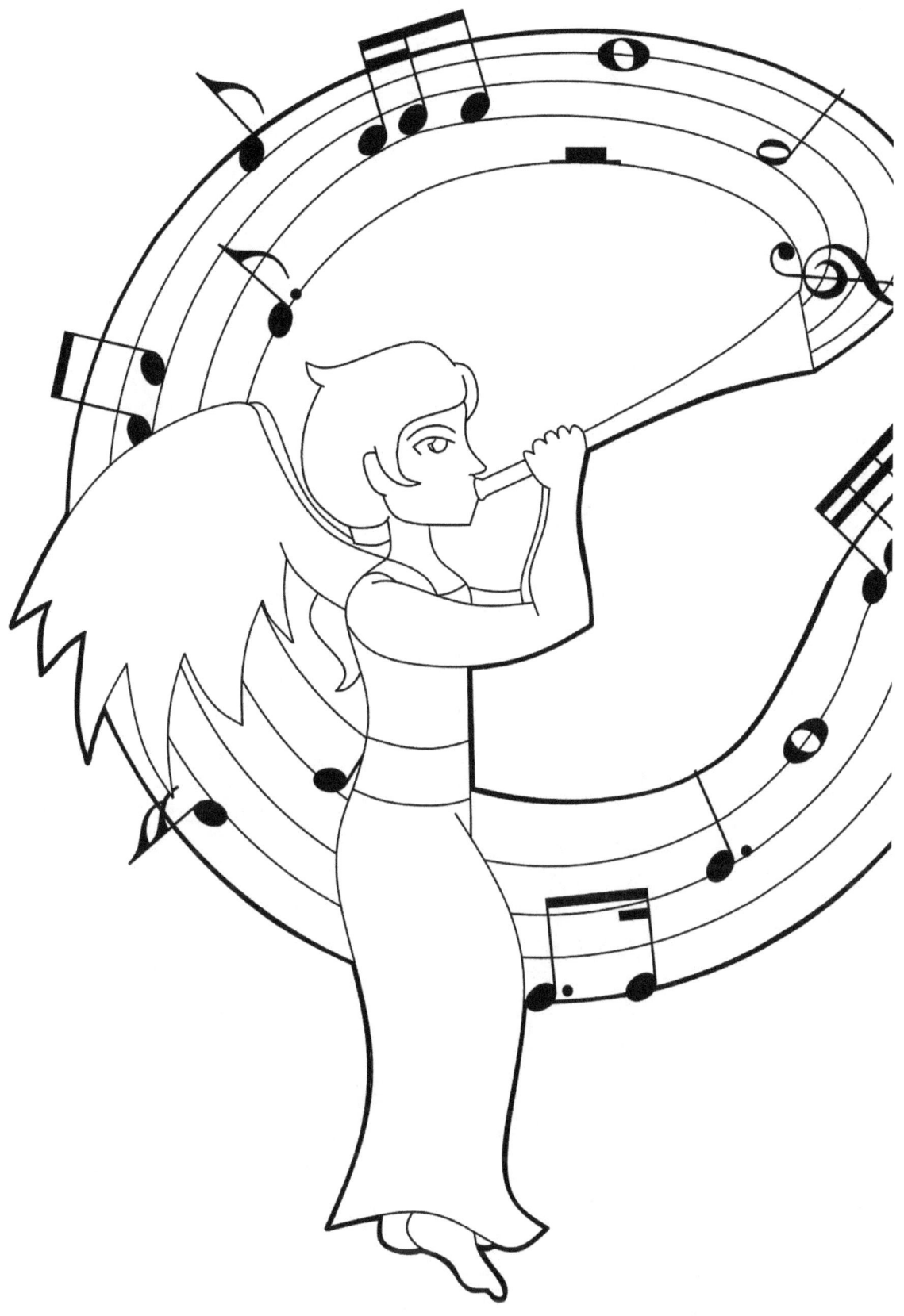

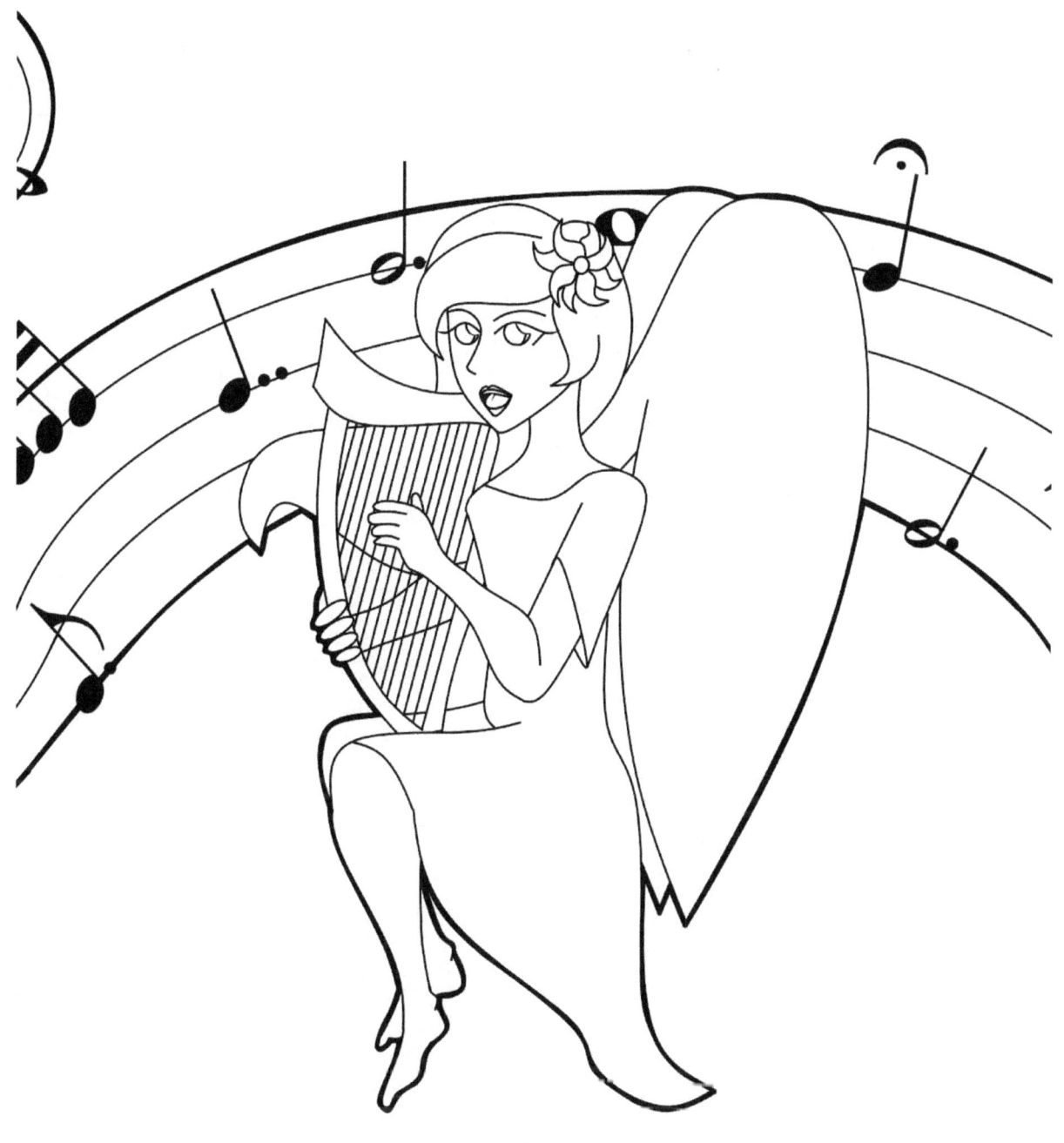

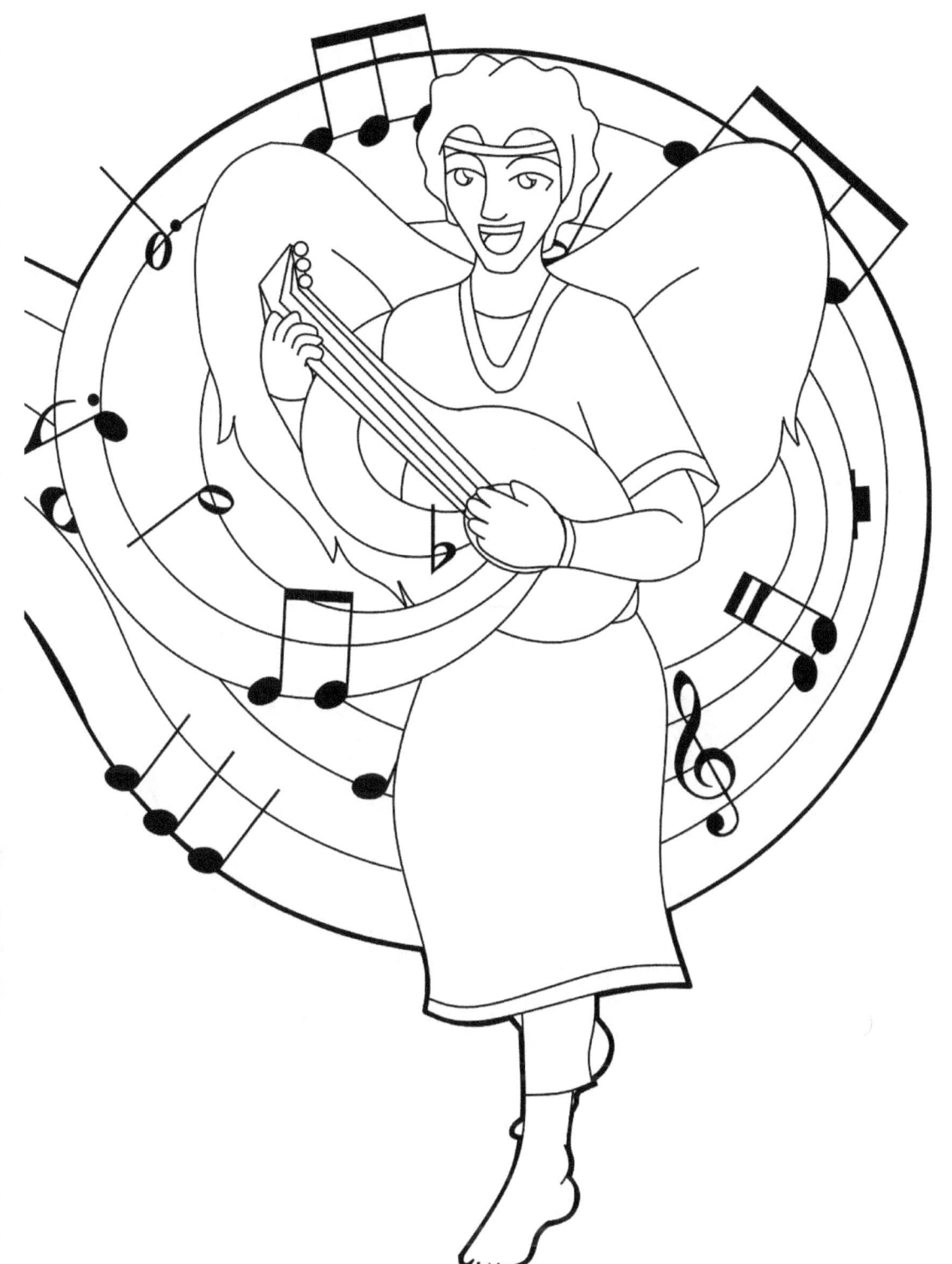

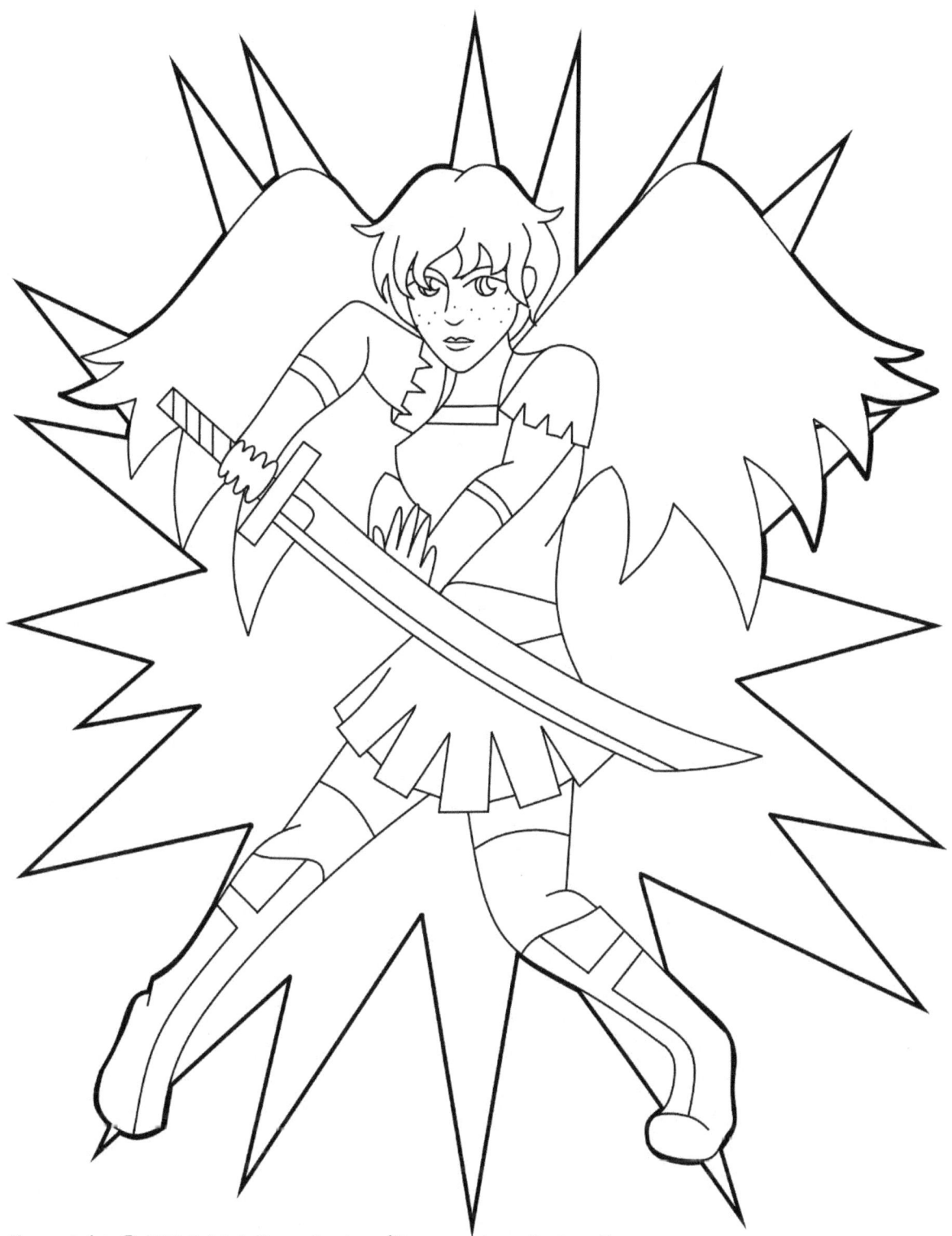

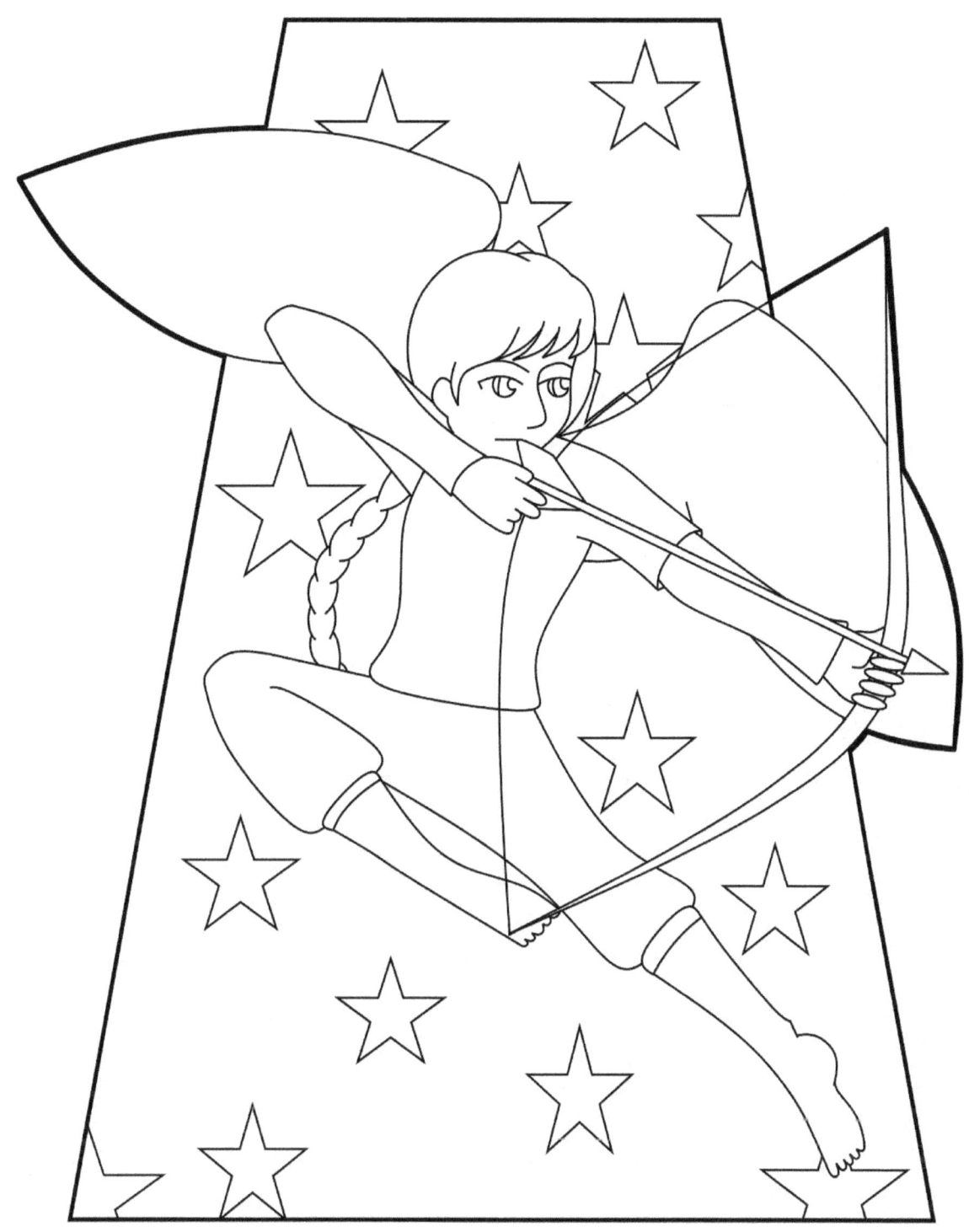

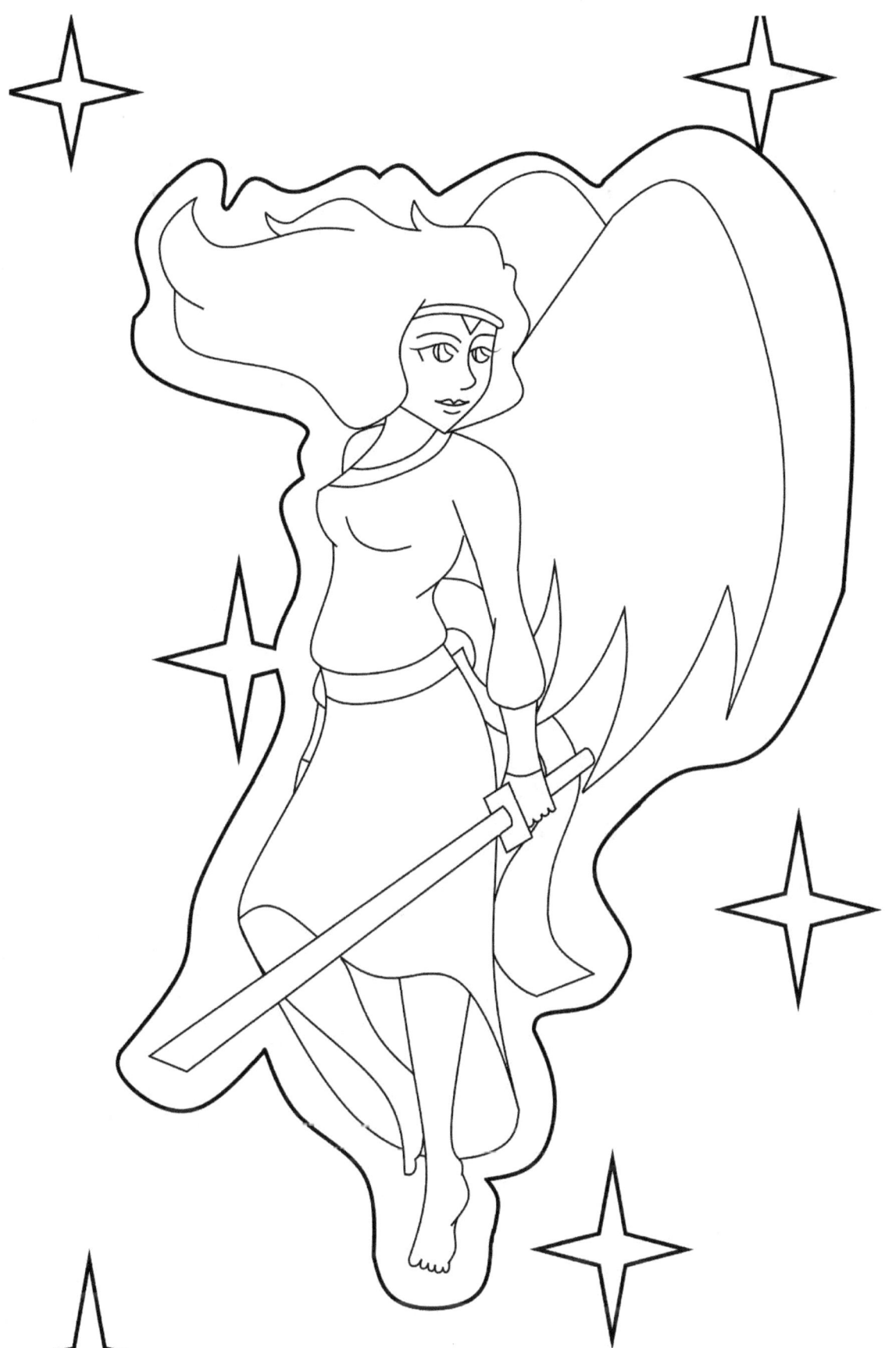

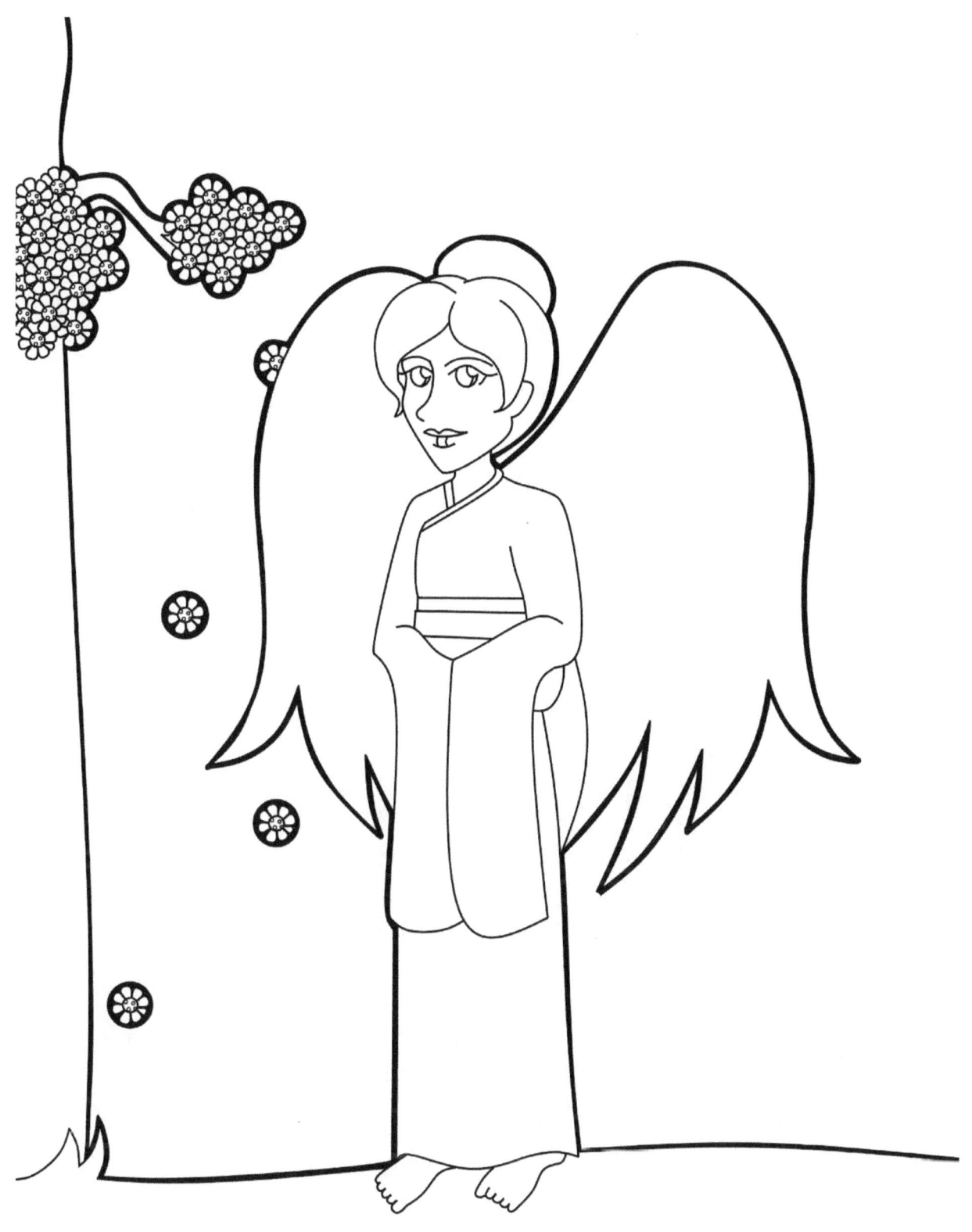

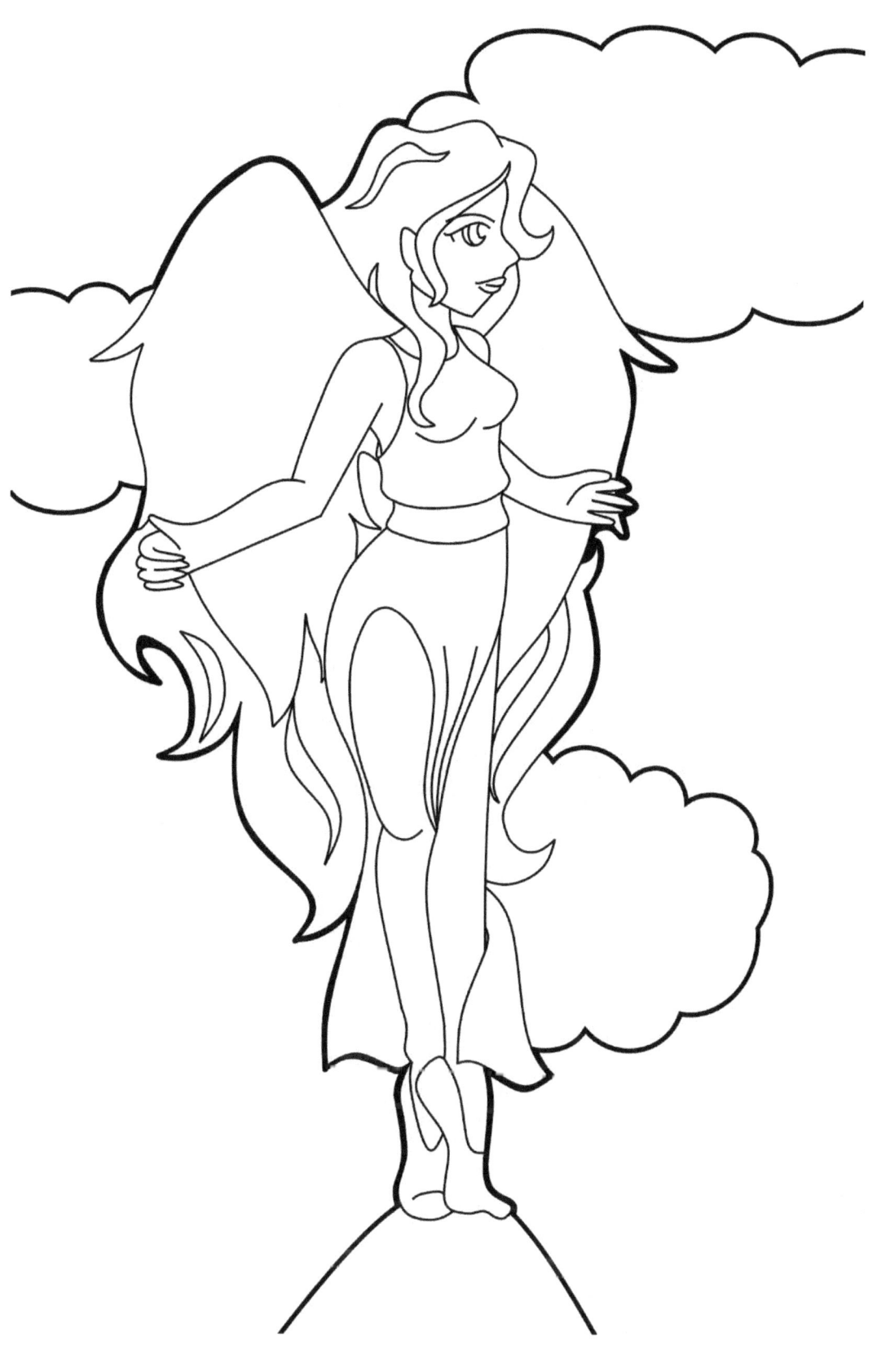

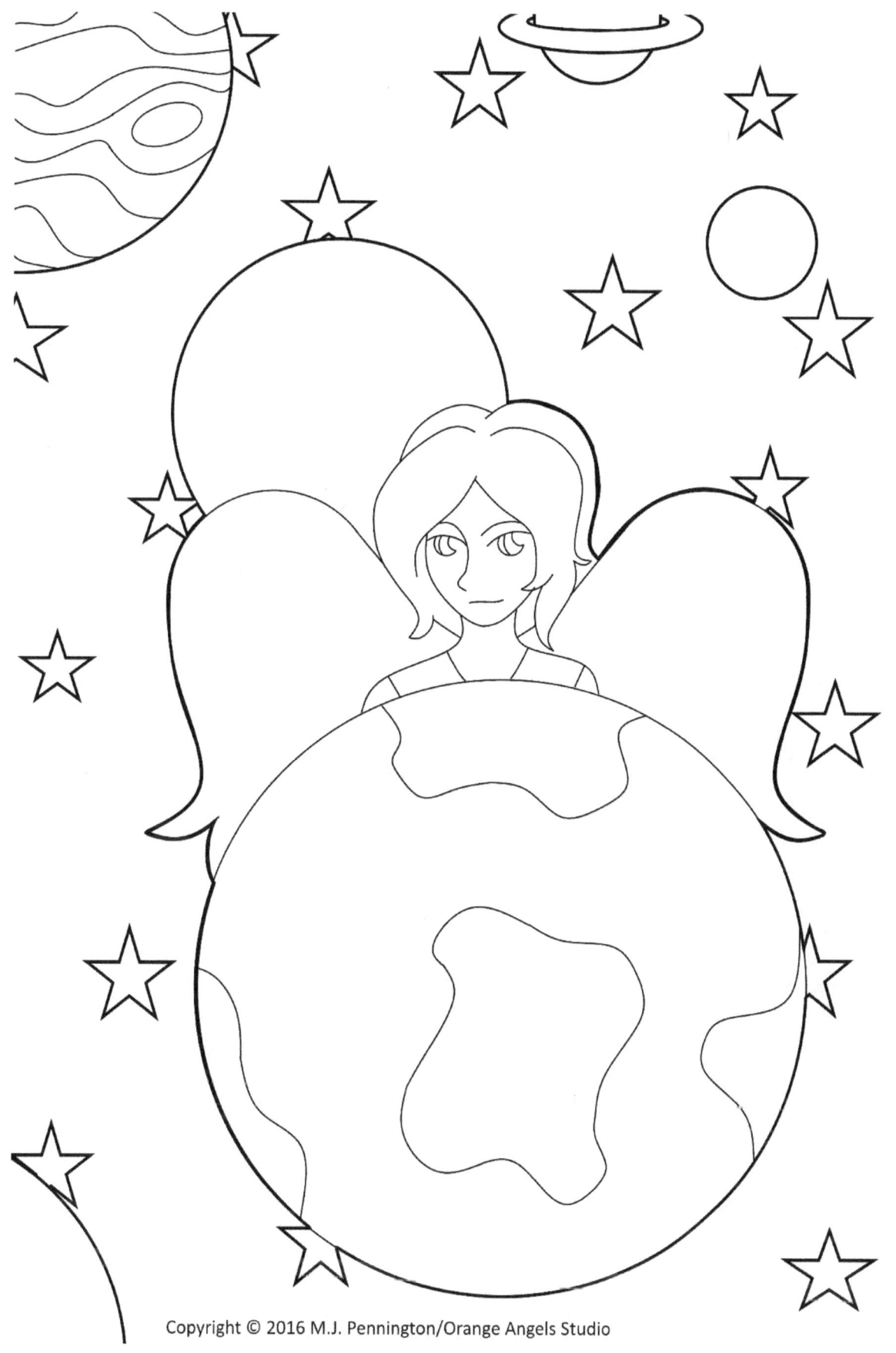

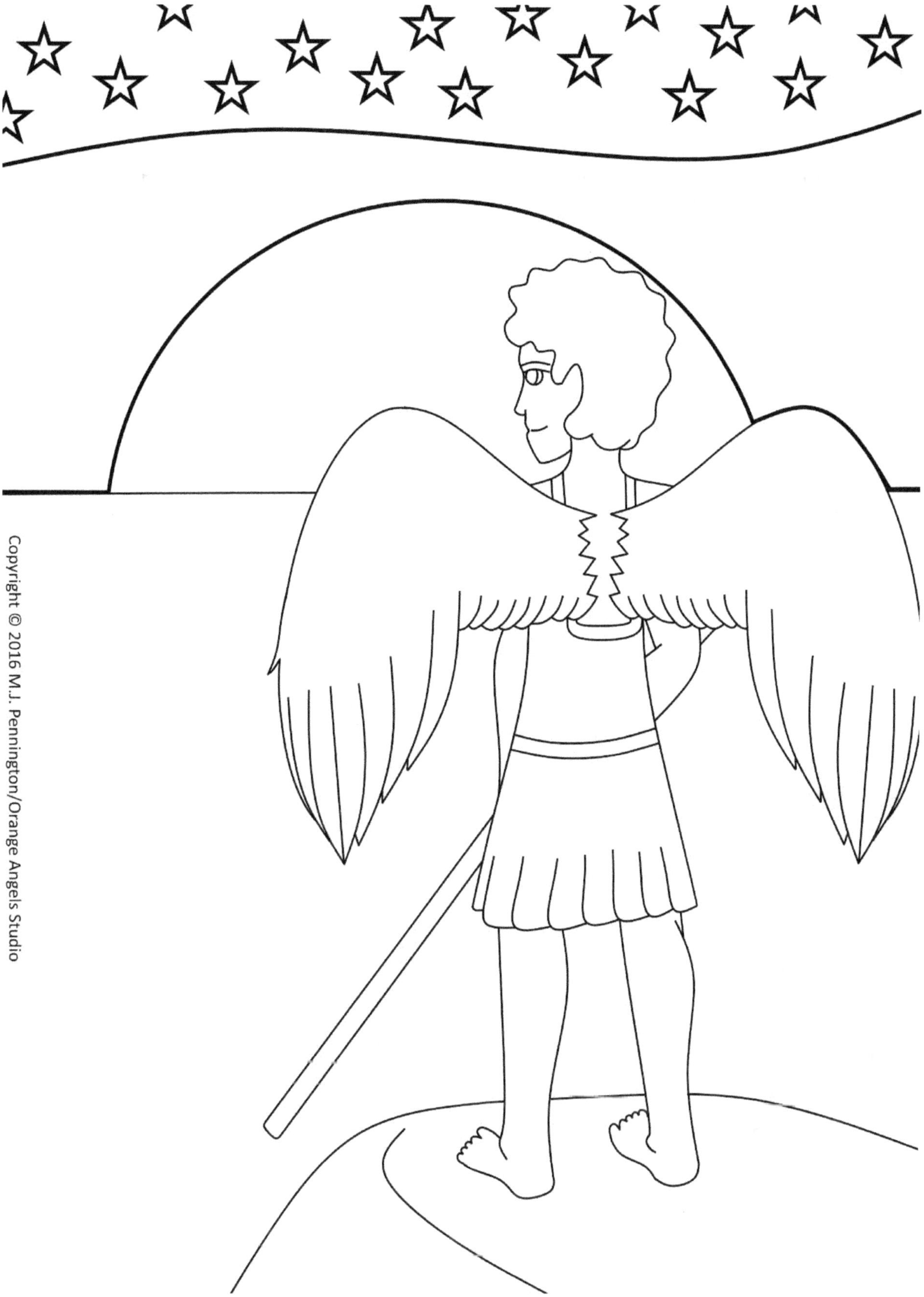

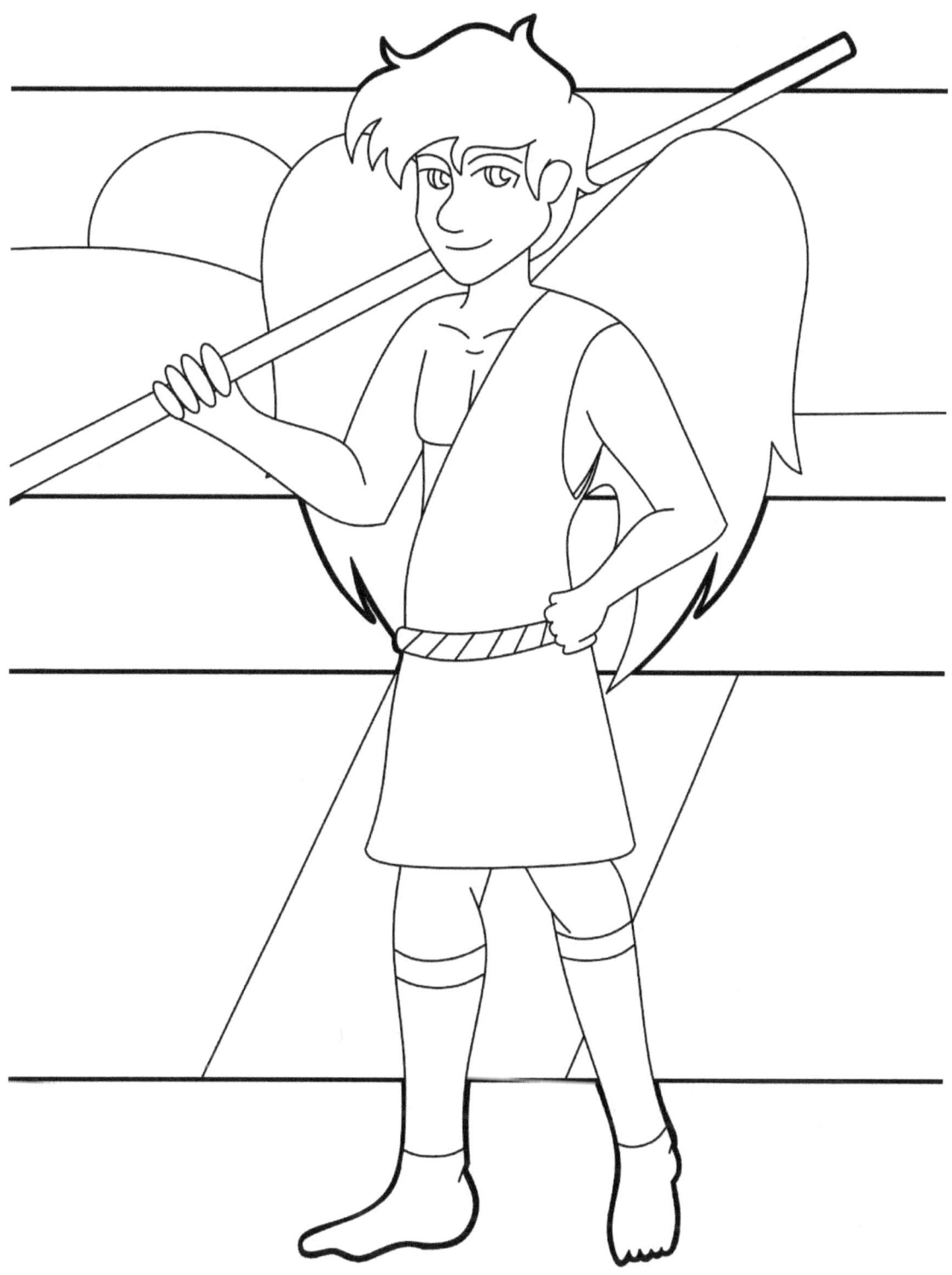

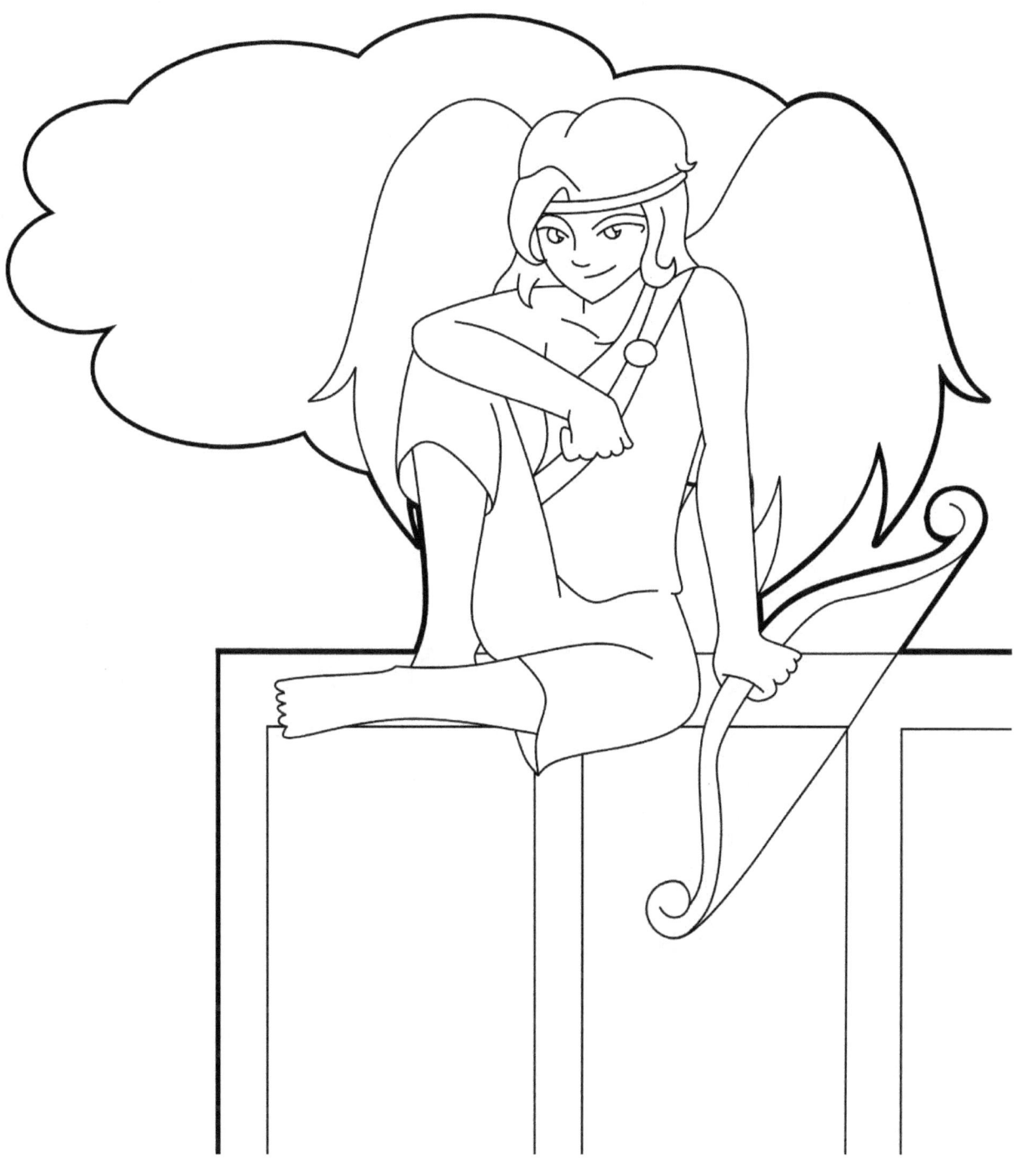

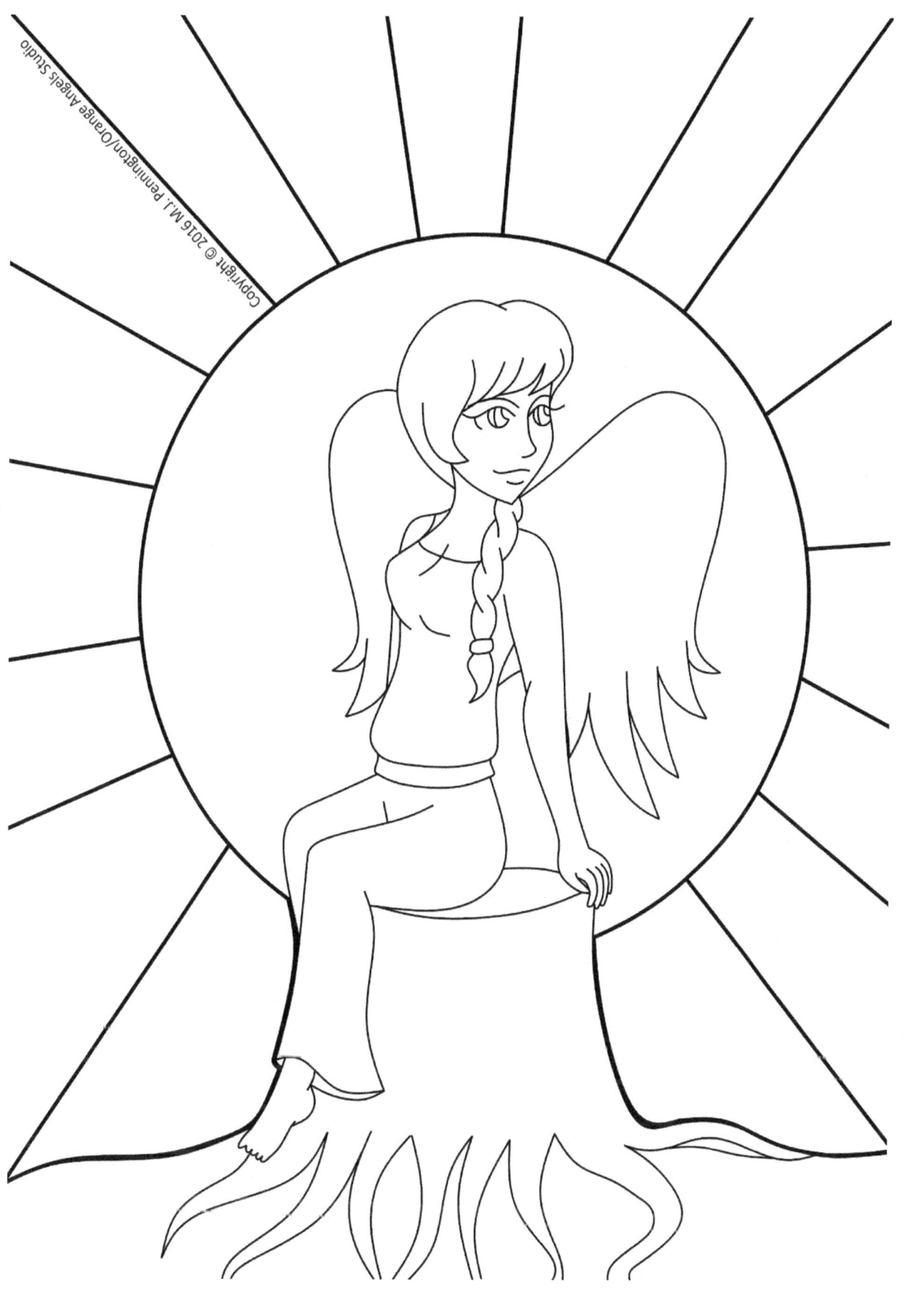

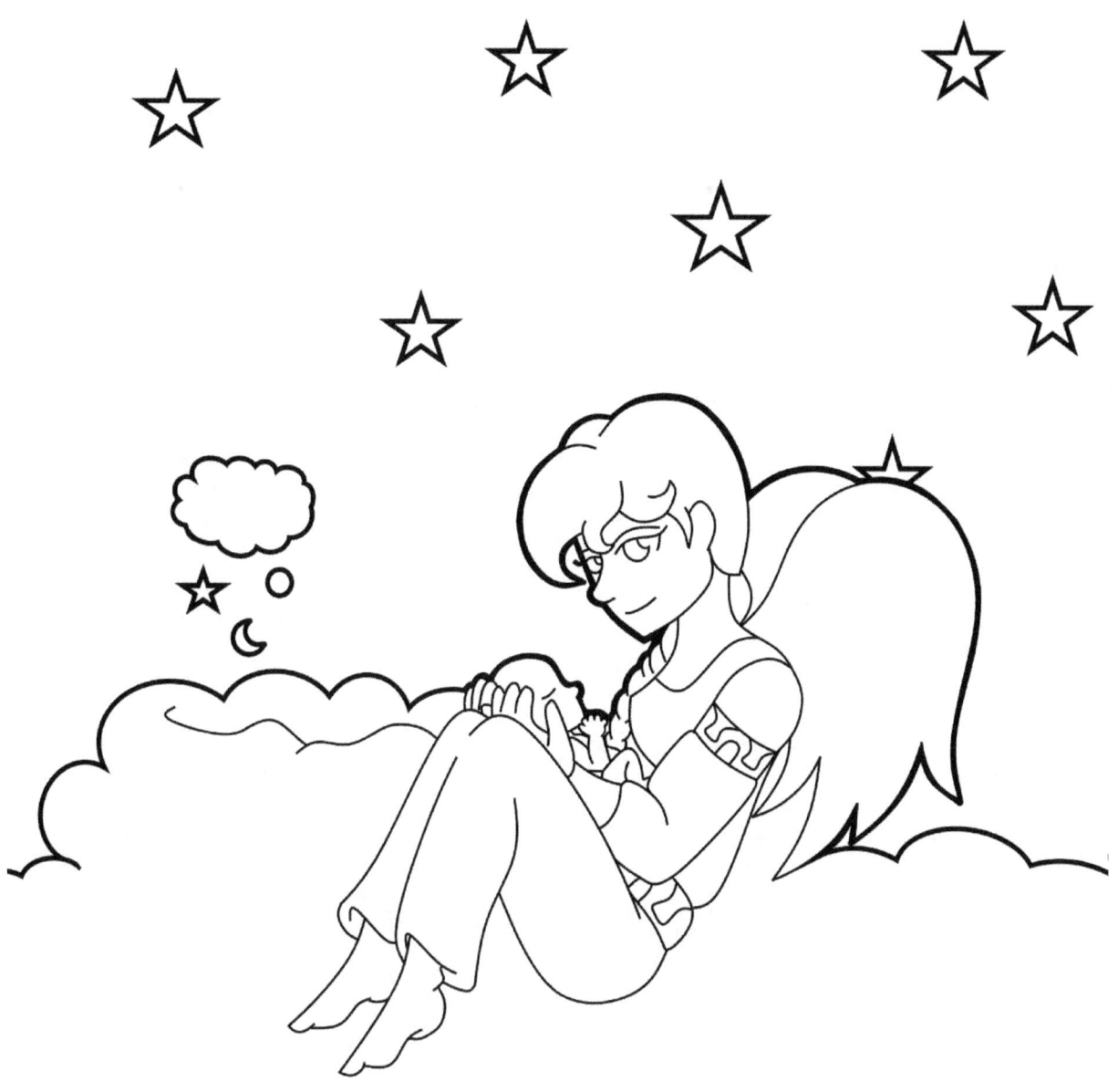

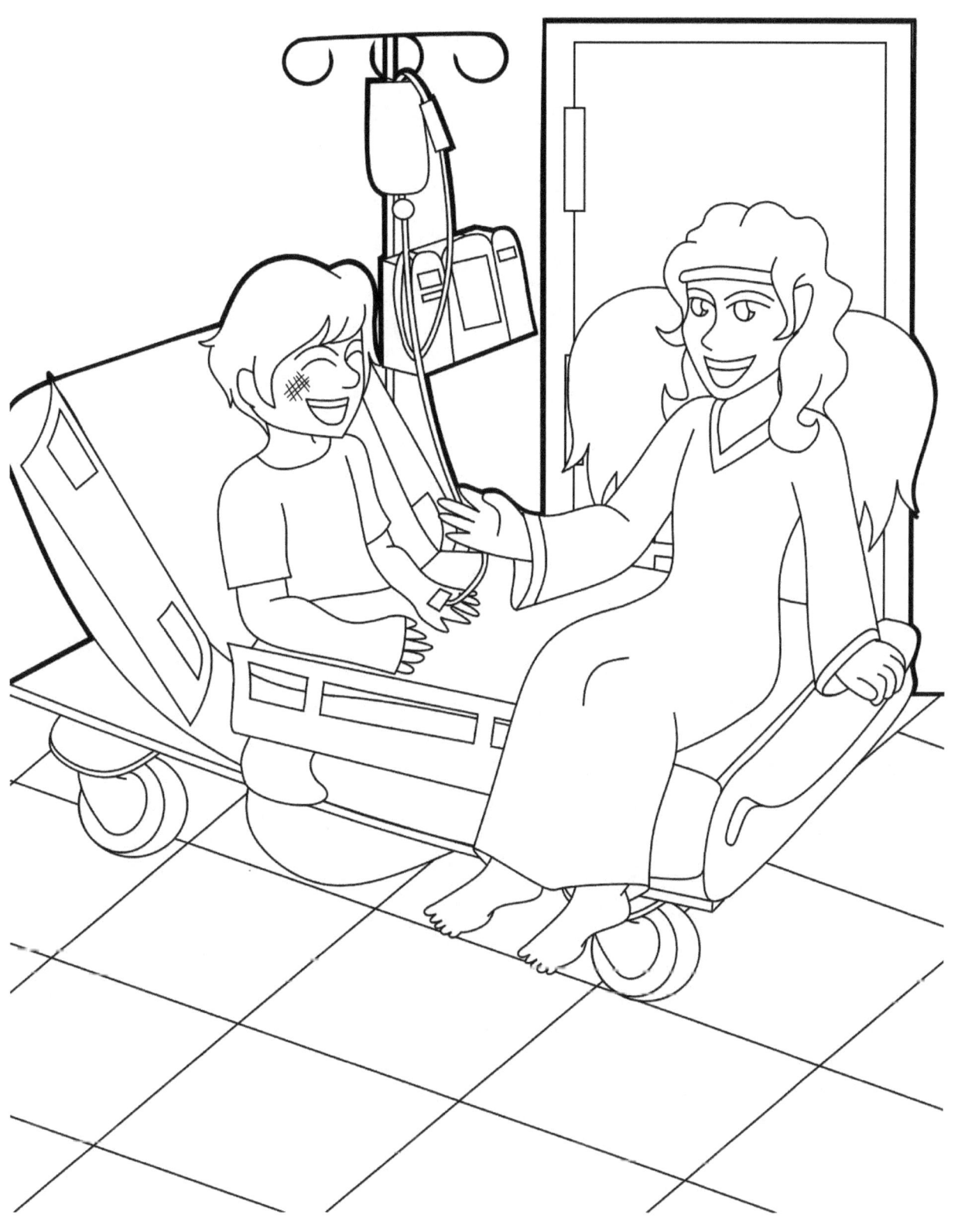

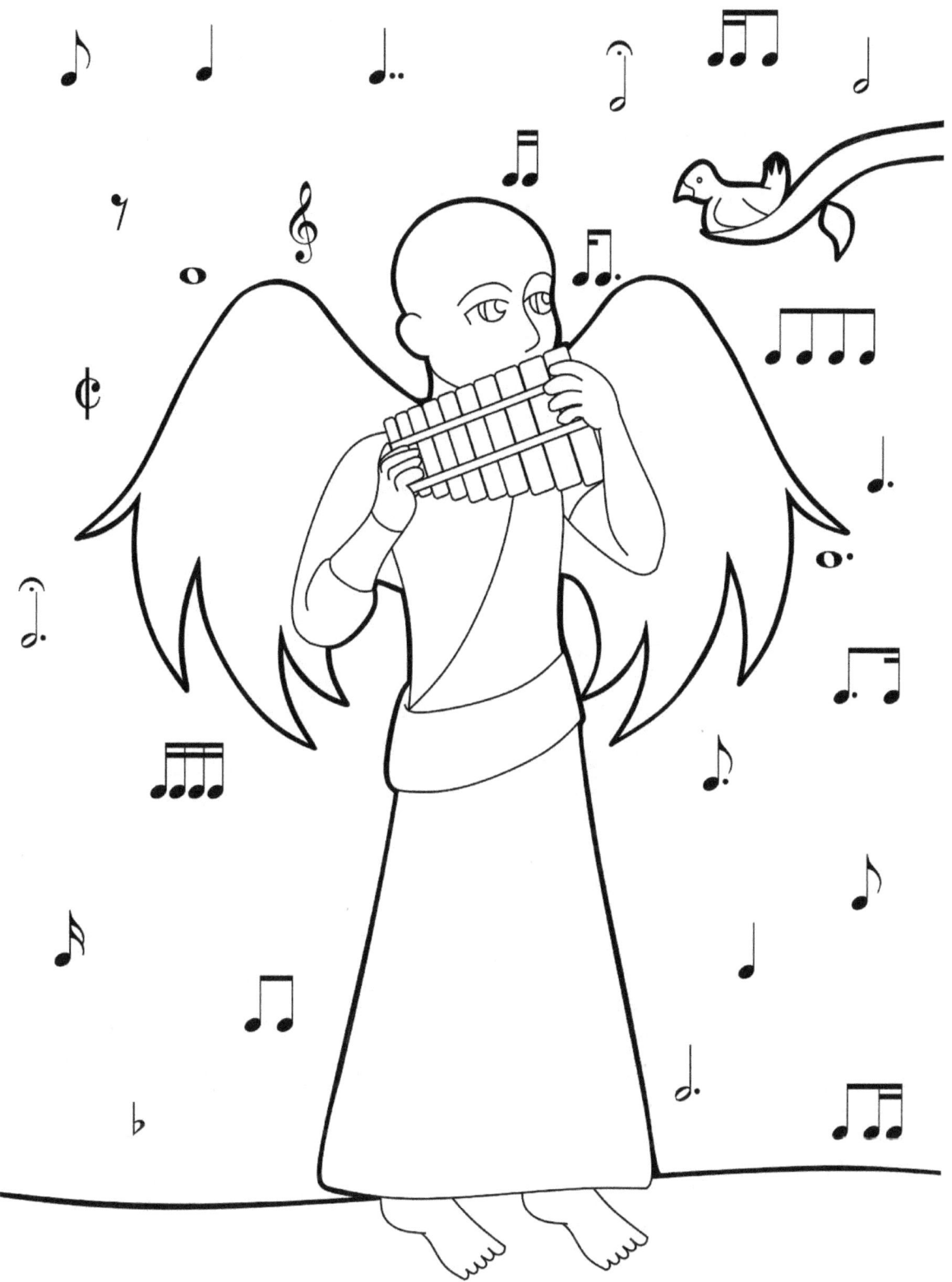

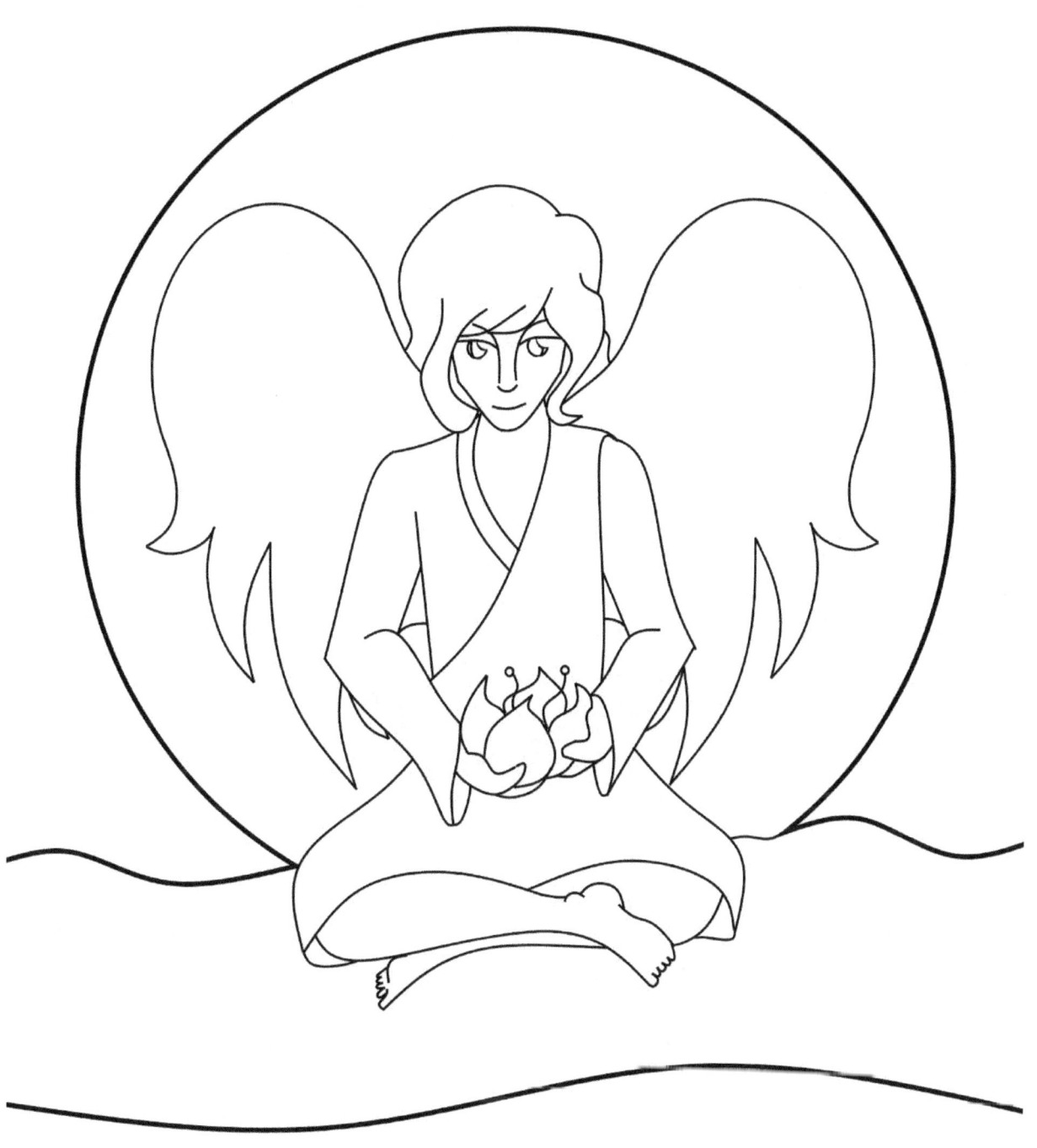

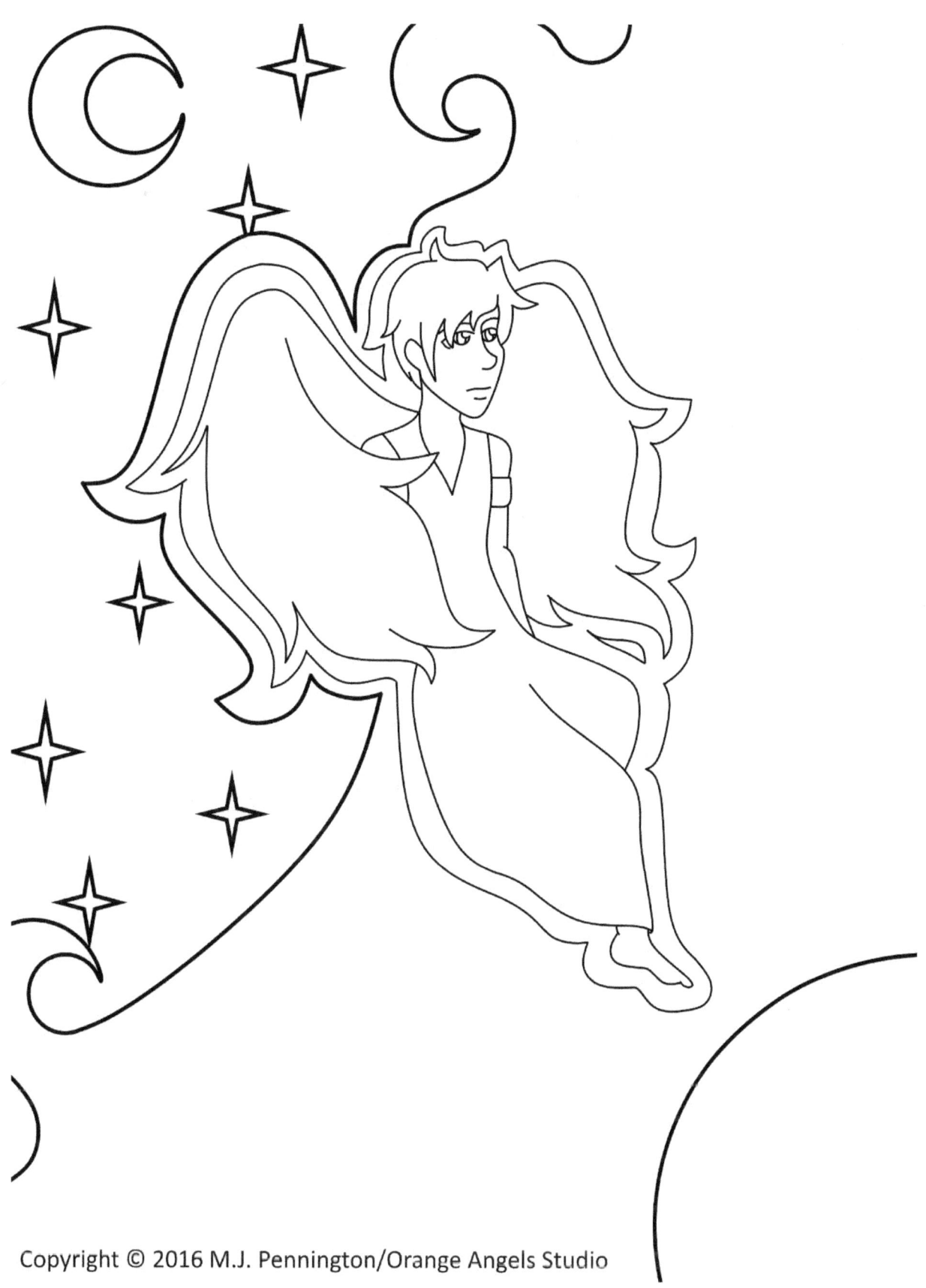

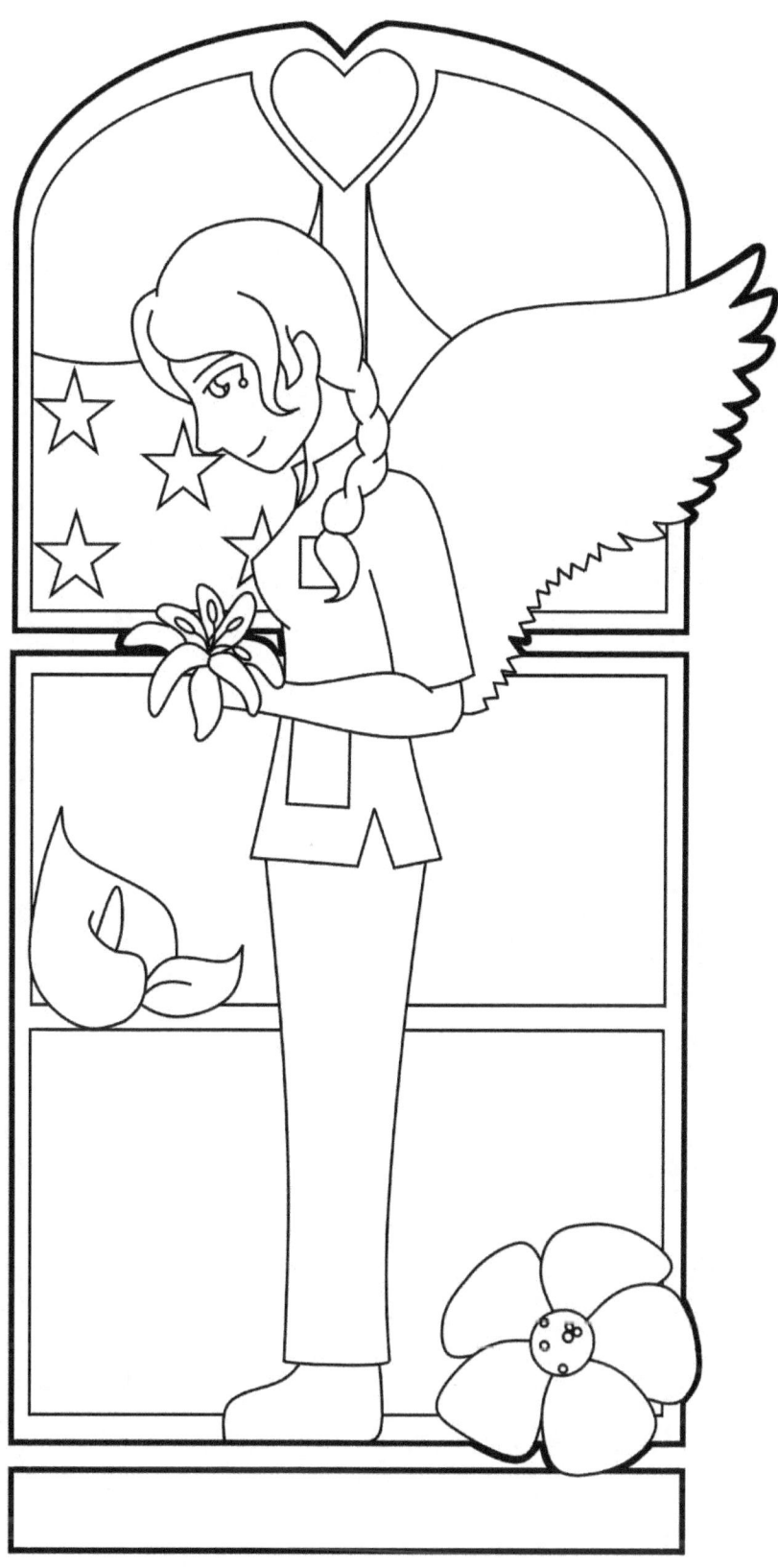

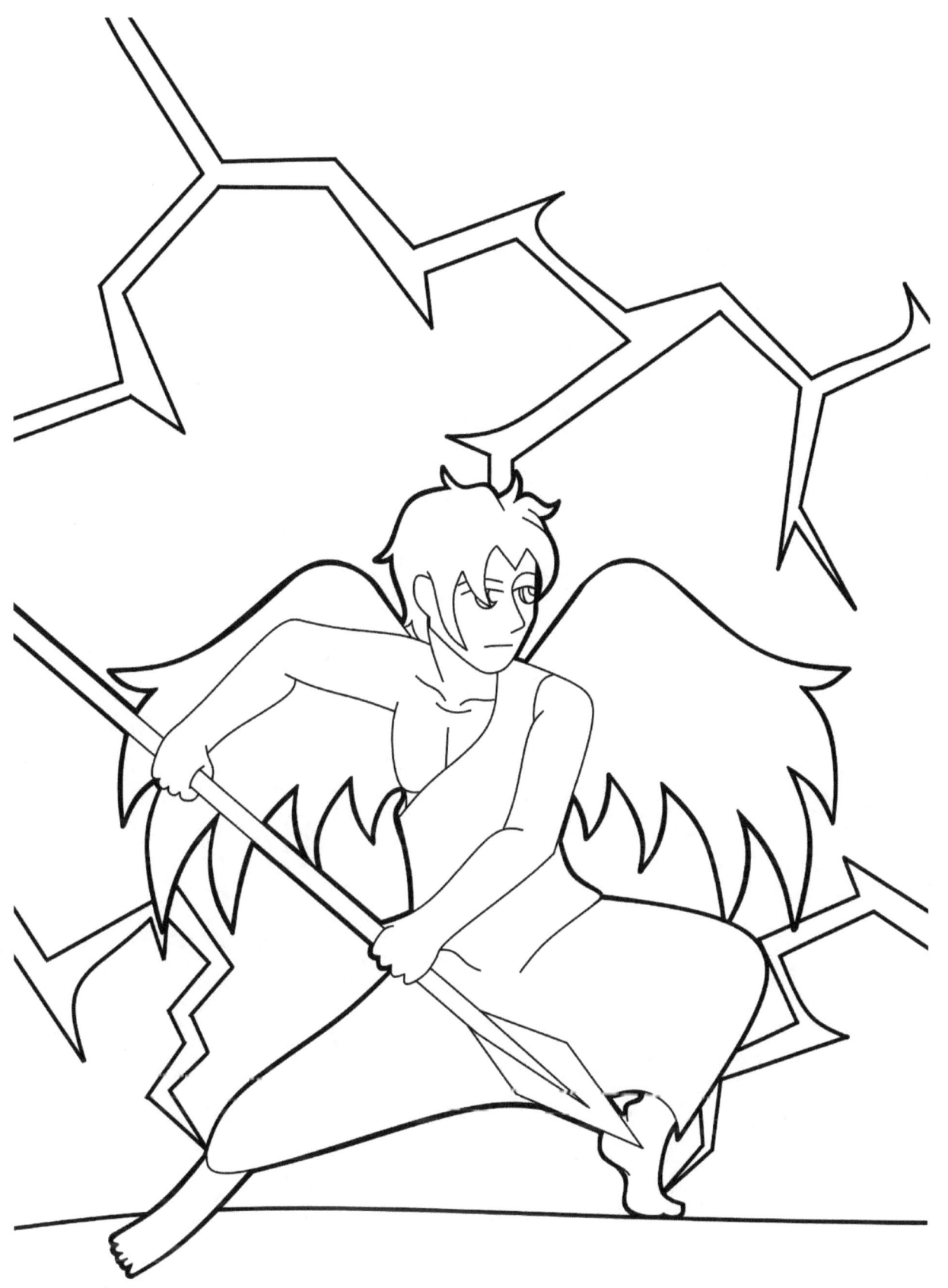

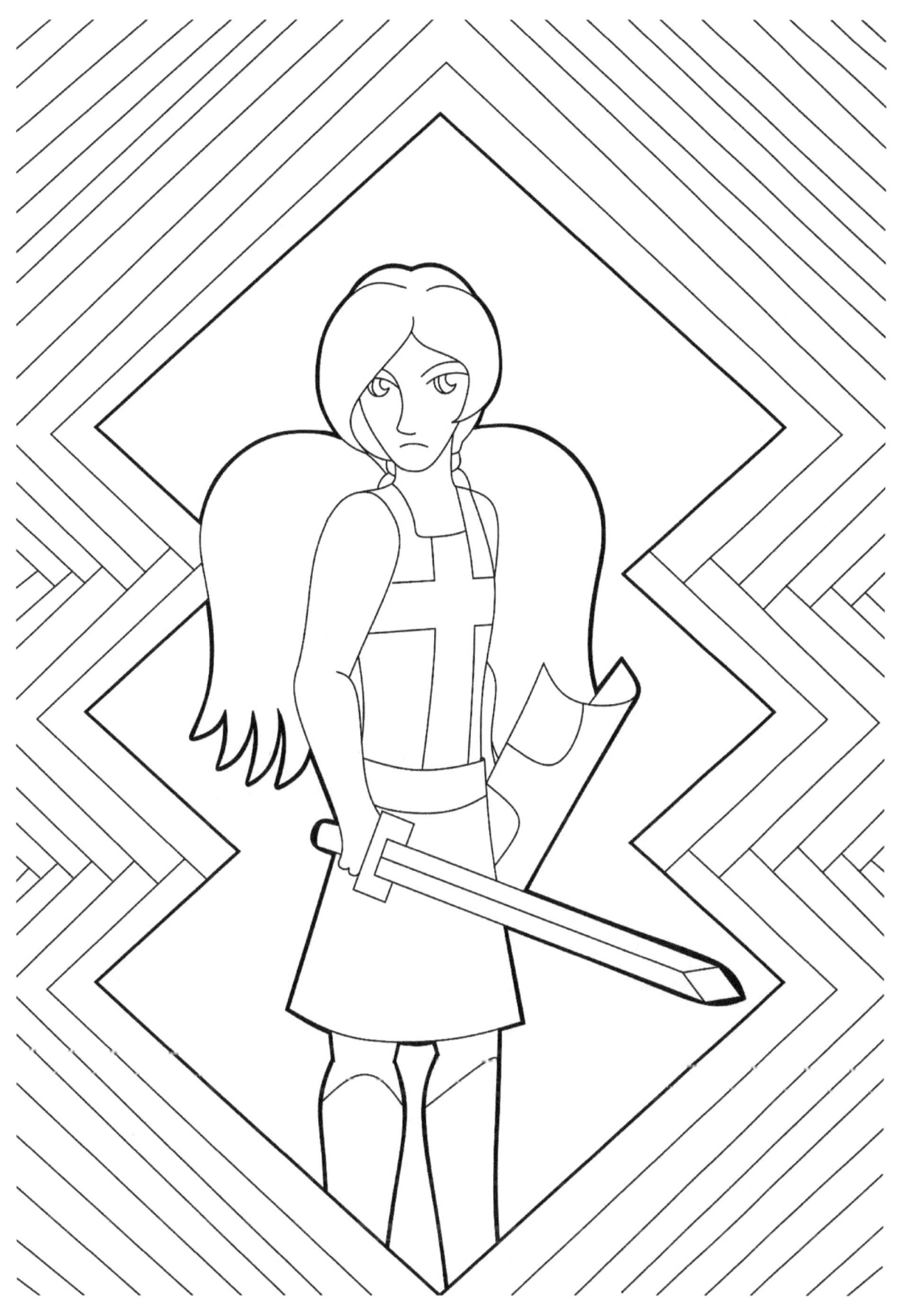

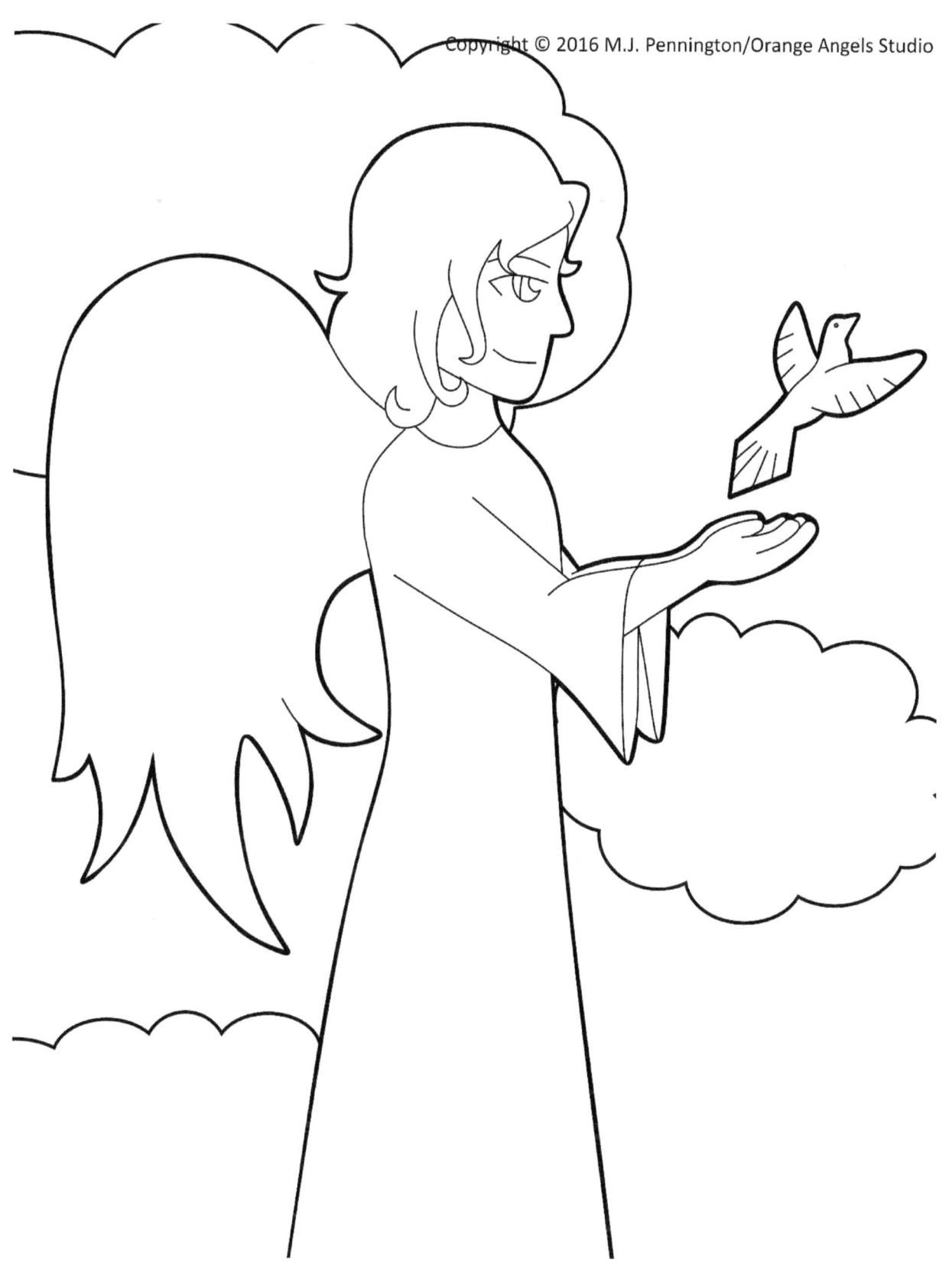

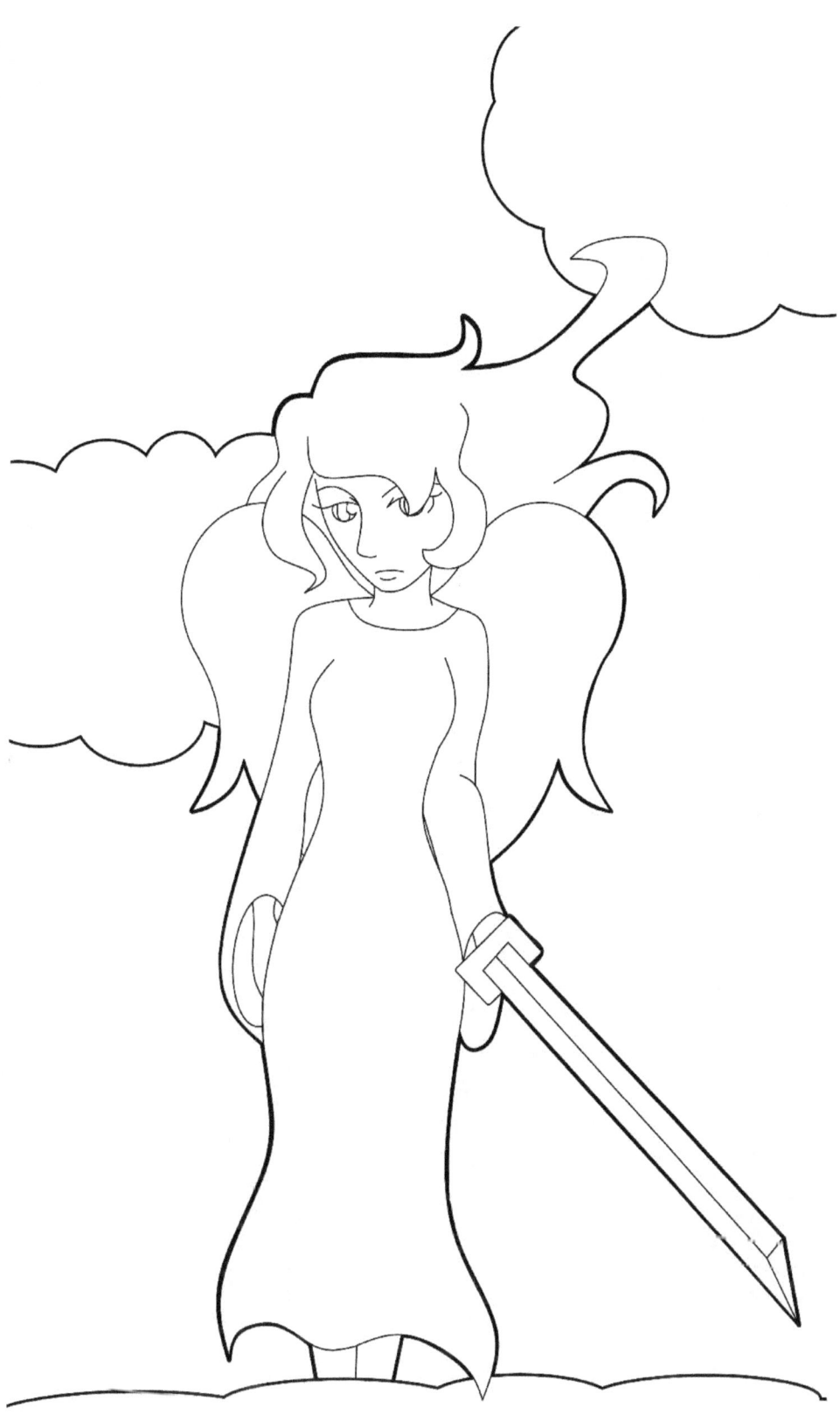

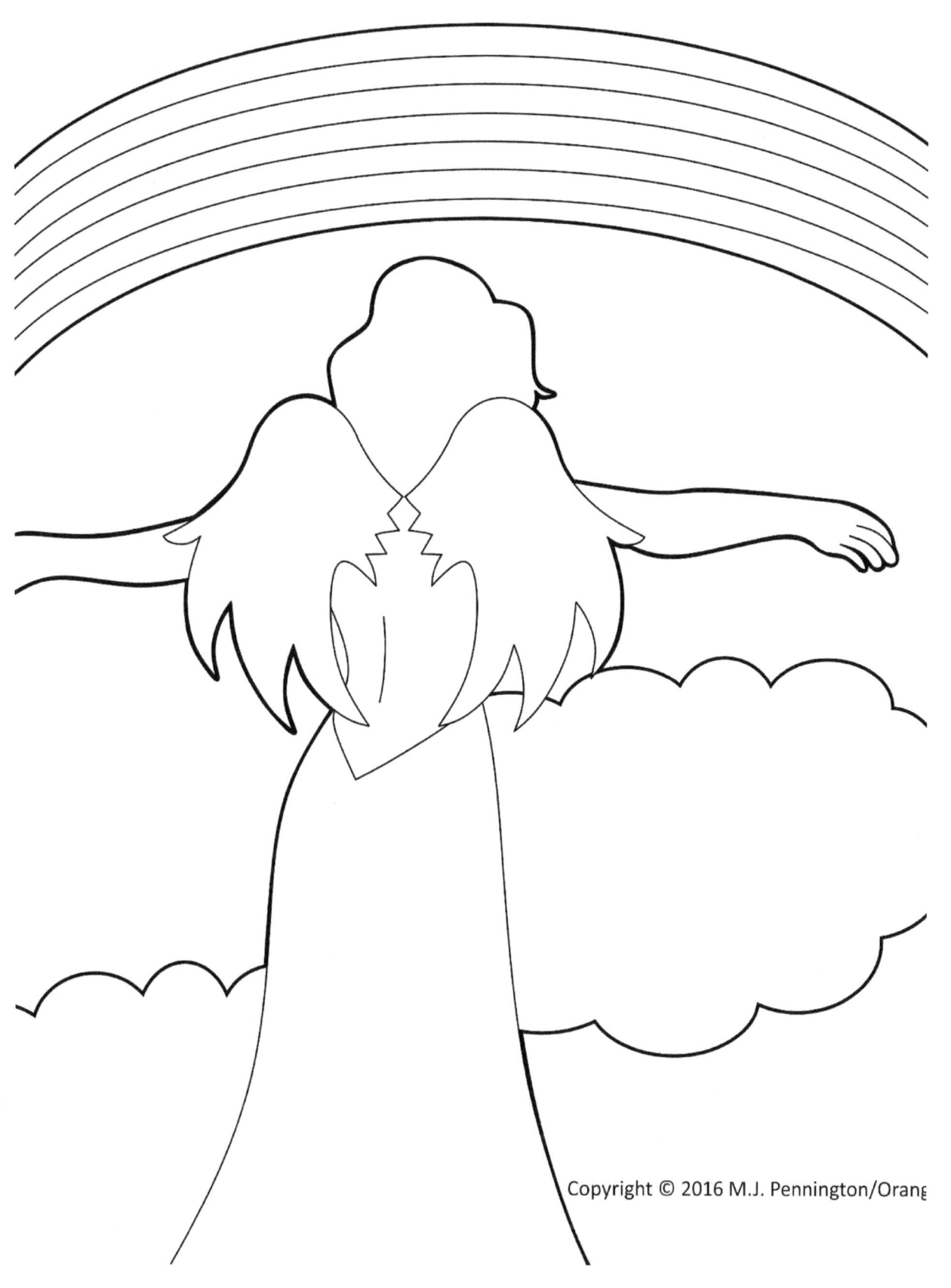

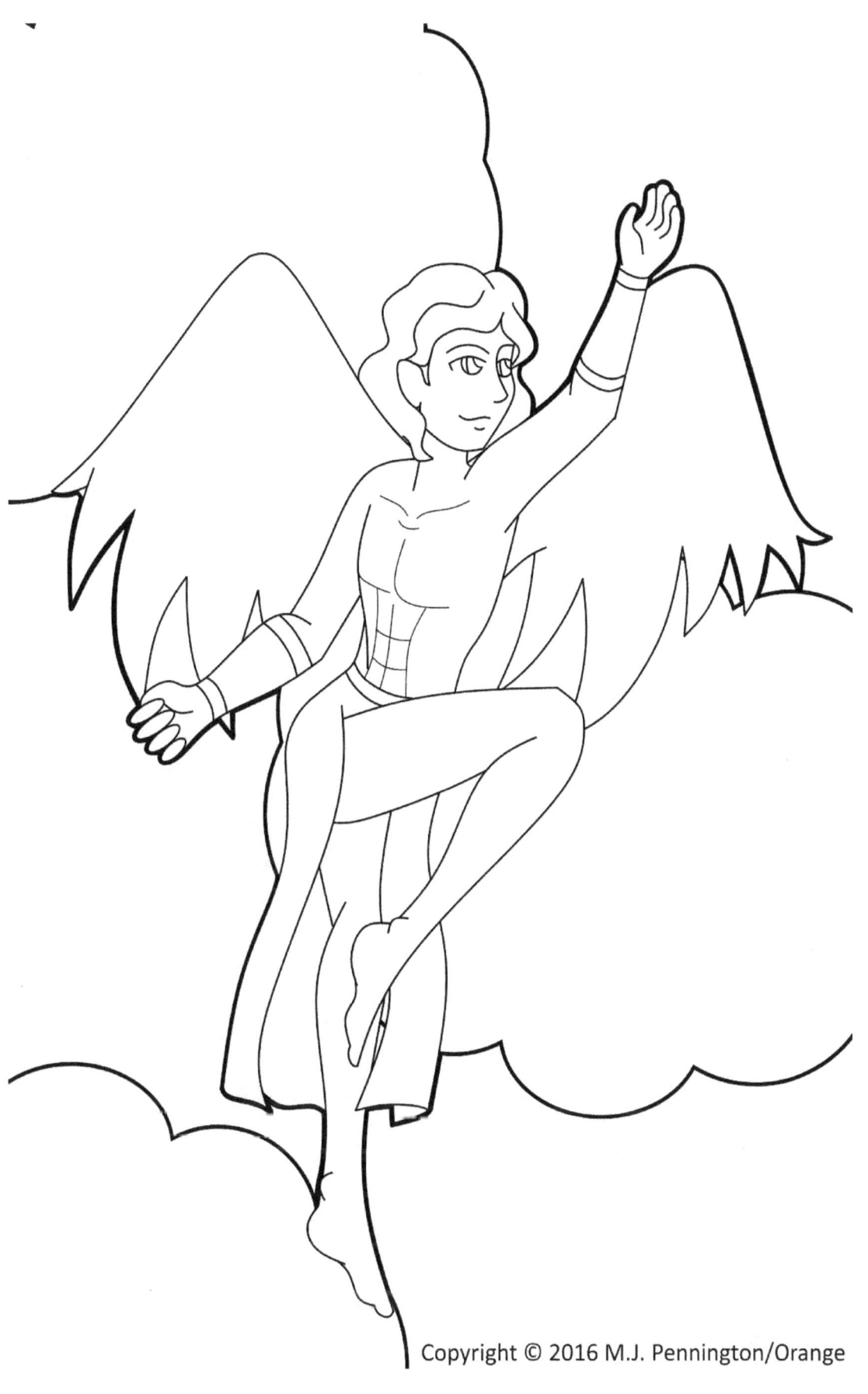

www.ingramcontent.com/pod-product-compliance
Lightning Source LLC
Chambersburg PA
CBHW080722190526
45169CB00006B/2485